Don't Slip On the Soap

Don't Slip On the Soap

Andy MacDonald

Musson Book Company
a division of General Publishing Co. Limited
Don Mills, Ontario

First published in 1978 by
Musson Book Company
a division of
General Publishing Co. Limited
30 Lesmill Road, Don Mills, Ontario

Canadian Cataloguing in Publication Data
MacDonald, Andy
    Don't slip on the soap
ISBN 0-7737-0037-4 bd.   ISBN 0-7737-1021-3 pa.
1. MacDonald, Andy   I. Title
FC2343.3.M33A32   971.6'95'030924   C78-001064-7

Hardcover ISBN 0-7737-0037-4
Softcover ISBN 0-7737-1021-3
Printed and bound in Canada
First printing

Dedication

Dedicated to the memory of my best friend, Ralph D. Currie, the burly Newfoundlander who was instrumental in prodding me on the path towards publication.

I Wish To Thank—

Rosemary Chiasson for all the articles she did on me, and her encouragement and enthusiasm.

Patrick Chambers, whose excellent cartoons accompanied my writings in newspapers and magazines.

Ed Suchenecki, who has taken more photographs of me than anyone else, and who did the photograph on the cover of *Bread and Molasses*, and this book too.

Patrick Crean, my editor, for all the faith he had in my work.

My brothers and sisters, without whose antics neither of these books would have been written, and with a special thanks to my brother in Halifax, Teedy MacDonald, who did much to promote *Bread and Molasses*.

My wife Rhoda, who put up with my many moods, catered to my company, and did so much typing on the second book.

My daughter, Dianne Copp, for the re-working, revising and typing she did on both books, and to my son-in-law, Frank, for giving up his wife from time to time, and to my two grandsons, David and Michael, for letting me borrow their mother.

I hope I haven't forgotten anyone.

Table of Contents

Introduction

For those of you who read my first book *Bread and Molasses* and have been waiting for my second one, here it is. And for those who haven't read *Bread and Molasses*, my advice is to get out and buy it as you'll get a clearer picture of our family.

Now in *Don't Slip On The Soap*, I'm still born in Sydney Mines, Cape Breton, and believe it or not, I still have the same brothers and sisters.

There's Murray, my ever-hungry twin and accomplice in many escapades, as when in *Bread and Molasses* we accidentally broke Pa's new Christmas pipe, while having a secret puff.

In this book there is a whole section on the mighty mishaps of this daring duo, who are still patiently awaiting money owed them by the King.

Then there's Teedy the youngest boy, who would burst into tears if you looked at him too long, and who in the first book was my partner in the big business venture of the "Pregnant Hen". In this book we still have the brains of a hen, even knowing what they are thinking, and we are still desperately in search of a hen of any description, even if it turns out to be a crow.

And of course there's Billy the Debonair, who could charm Pa like no one else, and could convince him that in the coming week Tuesday was to be held on

Monday. Billy was usually the instigator in most of our escapades, though Pa never thought him capable of any wrongdoings.

Then there's Pearl, the youngest girl who, when it was her turn for the dishes, would squeeze the cups to pieces if one of us didn't volunteer to wipe them off.

Ma was our Saviour, always there when we needed her protection from Pa. In most families the kids take the tantrums, but in our family if we didn't toe the mark it was Pa who took the tantrum. Pa was an exorcist of sorts, not ridding us of the unnatural, but the natural. He did it by the sharp, shrill command "Go to bed", which we heard more times a day than Ma saying, "Come and Eat". He had to be called "Sir" by everyone but Ma. Ma died when Teedy, Billy, Murray and I were in our early teens, and Pearl was seven, and it was then we knew Pa was the Judge, Lawyer and Prosecutor, and we had to plead our own case.

I can still see Sydney Mines, as it was in those days. Across the street from the Post Office was the Cooperative where Pa bought ninety-five percent of our food, on credit.

Heading east towards Sutherland's Corner stood our only theatre, whose mammoth frame seemed to be frowning, as if to say, "Where did you get the six cents to see the show?" On the left was the scarey red town hall which housed the fire station and the jail. I was never too eager to look in that direction in case the police chief called me over in his husky voice.

In the shadow of the jail were the three schools, braced and waiting for my summer holidays to end so they could enjoy my company and my disagreements with the teachers once more.

Further on was the grey Presbyterian church, which

Pa forced us to attend three times each Sunday. Lucky pigeons that never had to go cooed and cuddled in the eaves.

The twelve of us lived in a red house on Shore Road, close to the cliffs. My older brothers and sisters had left the roost earlier, flown away and married.

So return with us now to those Pa-filled days of yesteryear, when you will be a witness at Murray's and my birth.

Andy MacDonald
October, 1977

Chapter One

How Sweet To Be A Twin

Look At The Gob On That One
I suppose the closest one to me out of ten brothers and sisters, at least when I was being born, was Murray my twin. Some people say they can remember their birth. I not only remember being born, but also the days leading up to our birth, which were one long struggle.

I remember I couldn't endure the sight of Murray any longer. He was eying me like a leopard waiting to pounce, and were those horned-rimmed glasses he was wearing? Treading water close by, he made a grab for me so I swam to the other side of Ma. Slowly and deliberately, like a hungry balloon, he floated in my direction. Taking an extra long look at my skinny twin, I was appalled, as he was billiard-ball bald with nary a tooth. The enormous stretch of his mouth was identical to that of a day-old grey bird; with one exception—once the mother bird has spit thirty or so worms into its beak, the tiny bird rests its gaping mouth—but Murray tackled everything and never rested that stretch. Once I hollered, "Damn! I've only got one leg!" when my hungry partner burped, throwing my leg back into circulation. This was only an inkling of his appetite to come, and I knew if we

1

didn't get out of there soon Murray would chew his way out or devour me. It was so crowded I swore if I could get on the other side of Ma, I would do my best to keep some distance between us even if I had to build a partition.

Using a breast stroke that Jacques Cousteau would have envied, I swam to the opposite bank, which to me looked like a rib. I don't know what I was wearing, but it sure felt loose—like a maternity dress or my three-hundred-and-fifty-pound uncle's shorts.

We were getting right up there in age, especially me, and had decided we had seen enough of this murky underwater world. I felt two, three, or even four days older than Murray, so it was up to me to get the show on the road. But what was I to do? There were no phones, the water was still high, and I hardly knew Pa —hadn't met him yet. It was a terrible night and Ma wouldn't keep still. I was sloshing around and Murray kept bumping me, as though he could stand no more. Another wicked thump, then another. A tug of war began. Murray had extraordinary strength in his feet; and the finishing touch came with a left foot to my rear section, which sent me flying. I was fortunate to land in the bed with Ma, and not in the pot. I thought it best to keep quiet about the terrific battle with Murray. They washed me and laid me in the warmest little blanket. I knew now I was turning a pretty pink. What a change from the waterlogging I had got with Murray, who was probably eating himself up by now. I think he was a reincarnation of Henry the Eighth.

I was beginning to get uneasy waiting for my hungry, sparring brother (he might have gone out to a restaurant). I guess they weren't expecting him. But just as I was about to tell them to begin the search, I heard the commotion. "What? Where? Look at that mouth and the size of those ears, and he's drooling too!" Then I had the first good look at Pa, who had a puzzled look when he saw Murray. I was enough of a shock; could he stand two? He left the room shaking his head. Now I could relax and I snuggled my bottom further down in that cosy blue blanket, hoping they'd put Murray's wet, red body in a blanket by itself, so he couldn't take those large leaps at me with his rough swimming strokes and swallow me whole.

He cried a lot more than me because he was scared, and also his eyes were much larger. He had been left alone after he gave me that tremendous kick, like the astronaut who waits for the moon walkers. Now as we go through life, and people ask me which of us is the older, I sigh, but usually admit I'm twenty minutes older than Murray, by a left to the rear, and by having smaller ears.

The Day Murray Ate The Fly-Pad

Murray was noted for many things, one of the main things being his ravenous appetite, which I had noted in Ma's womb. Sometimes this caused him some problems. Like the hot summer's day when Ma brought home a new invention to catch flies that had invaded our house. (Not that we had many flies. It was just that it was hard to get to the kitchen at meal time without being knocked out by their bomber squads.) The thing was a round dry pad, and below the skull and crossbones were the directions. You were to place it in a container and add enough water to cover the pad. The flies would then land on this molasses-looking substance to refuel, sup a few sips; then as if chloroformed they would keel over, usually onto the pad, and stick there, and sometimes onto the table which was most appetizing. Billy and I were the only ones who had seen Ma preparing the fly-pad. Ma decided the safest spot to put it would be on the dining-room table, which we hardly ever used, except when the preacher made his rounds. Night was coming, and Murray had just come in from playing outdoors. As he walked past the dining room, the dim light from the kitchen shone weakly on the table. Murray, starving as usual, and unaware of the fly-trap, spied the delicious looking concoction in the shadows. Sneaking over to the table, so as not to arouse other greedies in the vicinity, he proceeded to wolf down the brown liquid along with the lifeless flies like a hungry frog. Then he ran to the kitchen gagging like a person who had just swallowed dead flies.

It was a few minutes before he could speak to give us the reason for the white look on his face. "Good Lord," cried Ma, "he's eaten the fly-pad!" This scared Murray half to death. If it had been me who had swallowed even one fly, I would have rushed out and thrown myself over a cliff. For awhile it looked as though I was to be the only half of the pair left. Ma soaked the froth from Murray's mouth while Pa phoned the family doctor, getting fast advice about what to do. (The doctor told Pa he thought he was raising a frog by the size of Murray's eyes, then went on to give some directions.) The cure was worse than being poisoned. Dry mustard and water was hosed down his throat, until vomiting started, and things came up that he hadn't even eaten. Not long after the half can of mustard was forced into him, a healthy colour began to wash over his face, and complaints of "I'm hungry" started pouring from him. I suggested he eat the rest of the fly-pad if he was that hungry.

Fly-pads were condemned by Pa, never to be taken into the house again. So two home-made swatters were quickly assembled. Murray recovered after a large meal of bread and molasses, and after practicing with the new weapons, he and I soon had the kitchen under control. There were a few arguments at times between us when we'd nail a pitched fly by taking a pot shot at each other's head, and many tempting moments when the flies were getting scarce and hard to find, and one would land on Pa's shoulder. It was all we could do to keep from taking a swat at Pa. But we knew it would have been our last swat, as we would have fared much worse than Murray after eating the fly-pad. Pa would have had us up for assault and battery.

If Murray Grows Another Head, He'll Have To Eat Twice As Much
Another time we almost lost Murray was the summer we were six. Murray was a great one for the dump. (If I hadn't been with him inside Ma I would have sworn he was born in the dump, or had sprouted out of a heap of rubbish there.) He could prophesy when a load of rubbish was to be dumped, and would be right there to have the first pick. One day Billy found him blowing in and out on a one-sided mouth harp he'd found in the pile, probably dropped by a poor angel who couldn't afford a big harp, and Billy told him he'd get leprosy for sure. Billy must have hexed him into a disease, because next day Murray ended up with scarlet fever.

Many a fright we got from a quarantine sign. Seeing this sign on a house scattered us to the other side of the street, not breathing in too much in case a germ had crossed the road and was waiting to enter our nostrils. Now here we were watching the health man hammer this yellow and black sign on our door. We felt like hammering the man, as this meant thirty days

5

sentencing to the house, a stricter penalty than Pa ever imposed on us for truancy. Murray was the cause of it all; and Billy, Teedy and I had little pity on him, feeling he'd messed up our lovely warm nights playing with the other kids. They should have quarantined Murray in the dump where he had picked up the fever in the first place.

Keeping Murray isolated wasn't too hard as he was too sick to argue. Ma's job was to keep us clear of him. Ma thought she had given us a good warning to stay away from Murray, but little did she know that we'd slip into his room and eat what he'd left during his fever, which wasn't much as no matter how fevered he got he still knew where his mouth was. We had no qualms about eating his leftover food, but when it came to a fork, spoon, or cup he'd been using, that was another story. A sneaky brother would wait until you had nearly finished drinking, then say tauntingly, "That's Murray's cup and it hasn't been scalded yet," having been told the germs jumped from the food to the utensils. But we gave them little time to make the leap. Spitting until your throat squeaked, you knew you might be the next victim that very second, and it took a lot of self-control to keep from running to Ma crying, "Put me to bed, I've got it, I'm turning scarlet."

I don't know why Teedy, Billy and I didn't contract the fever as we were surrounded by it. Our two sisters and two older brothers came down with it. Our brothers upstairs in a darkened room would pass chunks of hard candy they were eating down through the chimney hole. We'd rub the bite mark off with the cuff of our sweater, and into the mouth it would go, fuzz and all. Then we would desperately await the symptoms after the sweet taste left our mouth.

But Murray had that fever worst of all. And he was never husky. A week after he caught it, Ma carried

6

him out on a pillow to see us, and we could have done without that. I've seen sandpipers that had more meat on them than he did, and at least they had feathers. Murray looked like one that had just hatched, fallen out of its nest, and landed on a pillow. There was no such thing as weighing him because there wasn't enough there to weigh, and the scales flickered at zero. He also developed a large bunion on the left side of his throat, which was about the healthiest part left of him. (We thought he was growing another head.) Ma told us again not to touch him or have him blow his breath on us, which even without the fever wouldn't have been so fragrant anyway. So she didn't have to warn us, as he was about the ugliest thing we had ever seen.

We younger boys didn't catch the fever but we were a bit disappointed because of all the attention Murray got. We were the ones suffering the most trying to steer clear of the disease. I was positive I'd get it, as I'd been told that whatever my twin had I'd get it too, with the exception of candy, since he held the monopoly in that department.

After everyone was on the mend, our trips to the dump started again. As spring was approaching everyone was cleaning up their germs, but the ones who hadn't had scarlet fever were still very careful. If one of us grabbed something nice, a brother would say, "That's loaded with scarlet fever"; and as fast as we'd picked the thing up we'd throw it away. Then Billy would get Murray to pick it up, knowing that he was safe from the fever. This went on for a few months, and then it was every man for himself. Whatever you grabbed, you kept, scarlet fever and all.

Our First Train Ride
The first time I can recall being glad I was a twin was

once when Murray and I were four. Ma and Pa decided to take us on a train trip, about eighteen miles from home, probably to show us off a bit. This was the same as taking a trip around the world to us today. We were in ecstasy thinking we would soon be on a real train, that thing that gave a screech now and then miles from our home.

The night before, Ma almost tore us apart preparing for the trip, but we wouldn't have made a whimper even if she had caught the cake of soap in our ear; and I know I had two miniature heart seizures that night. Shining like new marbles, we thought of the trip all night long. Next morning, breakfast wasn't much needed (and that was saying something, especially for Murray) as the feeling in our hearts satisfied our appetites.

Dressing us exactly alike, Ma had a new little pair of pants, white shirts and bow ties for each of us. Why even if we didn't make the train that morning we'd be a dream to look at, strutting around the house all day. Any talent scouts in the vicinity of the train would probably have signed us up for Broadway on the spot.

We shunned Pa as much as possible because with everything going so smoothly anything could happen. The bottom might fall out of our cup or the yolk of an egg blob on our coats, or we could have been struck by lightning. And that would have been the end of our trip. In fact punishment for such an offence would probably have meant Pa declaring all trains off limits to us for the rest of our lives.

So off we went to the station holding back strains of smothered laughs in case Pa sent us home to undress and go to bed. We were very careful not to kick a stone and knock the shininess off our new shoes. Bustling with delight behind Ma and Pa, I think Murray and I were even talking in a foreign language. Glancing at Murray, I knew without asking that I was just as dressy and sexy-looking in the tight-fitting clothes as he, though my one cuff was a mite longer than the other. But this was only noticeable when I was at attention which was pretty rare.

On board the train our heads were like windmills, to and fro all the time, watching hydro poles race past the window. If there is such a thing as explosion of the heart from over excitement, we experienced it the moment Ma took us into the diner. It was beautifully lighted, and the waiters in white coats were almost more than we could stand. Ma ordered a bowl of soup for herself, winked at the waiter and he brought her three packets of soda crackers. This was high living. Crumb by crumb we devoured the soda crackers, occasionally accepting a spoonful of soup from Ma when the coast was clear. Why the prime minister couldn't have enjoyed a better meal than this. We felt so free during this meal as Pa had stayed in the parlour car talking to some union man. In fact we were in favour of Pa staying in the parlour car until we were in full bloom and married.

On the train ride home, unknown to us, was Johnny Miles, the Boston Marathon winner from our home town. At the station was a throng of people, a parade and the town fire engine all flagged up to greet him. Murray and I thought the citizens had missed us so much that day that the gathering was for us. We stepped off the train smiling, took a few bows, and were quite disappointed when they wouldn't take us home that extra mile on the fire engine, as we figured this was where the talent scout would notice us.

Once we arrived home, if any of our brothers or sisters spoke of trains in our presence it was a sorry time for them. The both of us at once would try and tell them about the inside out of the train, spitting and sputtering all over them, until one of them would clamp a hand over our mouth telling us to untangle our tongues. Murray could blow almost as loud as a train whistle, but you had to be on your guard against his powerful breath if he blew in your direction. We played train for years after that, lining up every chair in the house, one behind the other. Billy was always the conductor picking up the make-believe tickets. It took us about fifteen minutes to assemble our train, but Pa could dismantle us, caboose and all, in mere seconds.

The Cow Manure Facial
Though Murray and I were twins we didn't resemble each other much, except for a terrific cluster of freckles we had on our faces. Today freckles look pretty on a face, but we were splattered with them so badly our faces looked like maps of the Thousand Islands. The freckles were as large as small well-cooked pancakes and many a time we wished they would join each other and give us a tanned look to surprise those people who insulted and laughed at us. They never joined, but left just enough space to let the world know we had enlarged freckles covering every inch of our face.

No matter how dressy we got, which was practically never, we knew we were clothing a freckle. (We hoped as we got older, we would be able to get rid of them by pressing really hard on the razor as we shaved. We could shave our forehead and down over our nose, then snuff them in.) Everyone who visited us would remark under their breath about them; things like, "If they had another freckle they'd have to carry it in their hand." When we passed people on the street there would be an unkind smirk. Sometimes we'd rub our faces with a damp cloth, thick with soap, for nearly an hour trying to discourage those spots. Instead, after this hard pressing, they'd pop out like waxed chocolate balls. When someone called us "freckles" it was almost unbelievable the tempers we'd run. We used to hope freckles were contagious so we could press our faces against the ones who made fun of us, then step back and see their faces crawling with our freckles.

One day the manager of the theatre in our town put out a very interesting poster. On a dozen or more hydro poles was tacked the announcement of a beautiful show that was coming to the theatre, Stan Laurel and Oliver Hardy. We would have sold one arm to see a show like this. As it happened we were able to keep all our limbs, as this was one time Murray and I didn't have to worry about cost. Instead we had to hold our tempers because the manager was allowing anyone in who had a minimum of ten freckles. We could have taken the whole damn town in with ours. At the two separate entrances to the theatre there were attendants seriously counting the freckles on the faces of the boys and girls. It was surprising how hard it was to find ten freckles on a face other than ours; and they felt no qualms in turning away those who only had nine, and us with bushels to spare.

Murray and I decided not to go near the show until it was nearly ready to start, remembering the previous day when a group of school kids looked at the posters and then looked at us, saying in a very sarcastic tone, "Do you think you have enough to get in?" Like two experienced gangsters waiting for just the right moment, we walked toward the entrance as the manager was getting ready to close the main door. We felt bare naked as his eyes focused on our gingersnaps, and he said in a high-pitched voice, "Well, well, well. We've turned hundreds away. Had you come earlier, you boys could have helped them in with all your freckles." We felt as though he was hurling obscenities at us. We tried not to blush as that made them stand out more, if that was possible. He never bothered to count our freckles as we had more than ten on our left ear lobe, and we left five minutes before the show ended to avoid a ribbing from those who only had ten.

We carried those freckles around with us for ten or twelve years, and they got more plentiful each year. We use to tell each other they were hatching. Any cure to get rid of them was grabbed upon at once. We'd gladly have had a surgeon turn our cheeks inside out, as it was mostly on the cheeks that they hovered. One remedy offered by an old Irish woman (who at the age of ninety, we figured should know a cure) was to get up early in the morning, go down to the pasture where cows were kept and find a plop of cow manure, or cowflaps as some people call them. The small puddle of water in the center was supposed to be the first dew of the morning, bless the cow. This we were to rub on our faces, covering every freckle. That meant our ears too—every bit of our face in fact, except our tongue and eyes. After ten days they were supposed to disappear, never to return again. How we loved this old lady for ten days because of her magic potion. We carried coal to her back porch in buckets, cleaned her yard, fed her five black hens, and sometimes she'd feed us some rice pudding out of a baking powder can.

It was late spring and the few farmers in the village were putting their cows out to pasture. Murray and I never even let on to our brothers and sisters what we were up to, so disgusted were we with the word "freckle", it being a four-letter word to us. Murray and I set the Big Ben alarm clock for five a.m. for the first day. It didn't take much of a ring to get us out of bed we were so excited on this first day of the termination of our freckles. I'll bet you couldn't find many that excited about plastering cow manure juice on their faces. We made some oatmeal porridge, and after eating arrived at the old farmer's pasture. My first mistake was to back into a plop, turning my new white sneakers in to a dull summer green. The best splurp we could find was about a foot in circumference with a dinge in the center about six inches deep. Now this held plenty of dew. As it was quite a spill we used both hands, as if washing in a hand basin. "Pat it gently on the face for about fifteen minutes," was the old woman's instruction. With all the freckles we possessed, we knew we'd have to double up on the recipe.

At this early hour, even with no one around, we felt embarrassed as though we were performing acts of perversion when cows with muffled moos would stare at us while we were in the patting stage. We also noticed not one cow had freckles, so that was a sure sign this would work. Another part of the cure was to let it dry on your face for three hours. This was the toughest part. Sitting next to an unfreckled brother who wasn't pasted up, we'd be called everything but a rose.

Diligently sticking to the directions however, we never missed a morning for those ten days. No one would recognize us when this was over, not even the cows. Murray had a small mirror that he'd found in an old purse at the dump. He never carried this on his person, but kept it well hidden in the pasture in a good safe place next to a marked stake where the cows couldn't trample it, or cowflap on it. After taking turns patting on the cow-manure juice, we would analyze our spots in the sharp-edged mirror. It was very puzzling. Our freckles looked much larger after the potion was applied, but the old lady had said that the freckles would disappear by the eleventh morning and we wouldn't even know it. (If we survived.) Maybe she meant we wouldn't even know it because by that time we'd be unconscious from the smell.

At home we had a mirror which hung over the sink. The only way to get a good look in it was to stand on a chair. We avoided these conspicuous moves in front of the rest of the family so as not to be accused of vanity, but sometimes finding the house empty Murray and I would survey our spots. On the fifth or sixth day, we were hysterically happy. Looking in the mirror over the sink, we noticed the freckles were much smaller than when we had looked in the pasture mirror. However the next morning in the pasture our freckles looked gigantic again. But we passed it off by saying maybe they had expanded over night. We made excuses for the cow concoction, saying that that must be the way it acts, feeling the whole point of the remedy was for the freckles to become so enlarged that after the tenth day they would burst and disintegrate into the air. So we would reinforce the next mixture, and at home we were told we smelt like barn rats, looking like someone had just varnished us. Wouldn't Pa love to know we were mucking ourselves up with moo juice. If he had found out, we would have been banished to the cow pasture forever.

We hid an old towel in the porch and after each scrubbing we gave our faces we'd shake that towel desperately, positive there were some weakened freckles in it that weren't able to survive the freckle cure.

Finally, the tenth day arrived, and we were convinced that on the eleventh day we would surprise all mankind, and make headlines around the world. Next morning the chair was lifted toward the old mirror, and the face that peered into it the eleventh day was the same face that looked into it the first morning—no change whatsoever—just disappointment and our same small muddy puddles with high brown gloss, shining like polished brass door knobs.

With nothing to lose now but a carload of freckles, we made for the pasture mirror and found out why our freckles were getting smaller in the kitchen mirror. The pasture mirror was one of those magnifying mirrors that made the smallest face look large. No wonder we worked so hard in the pasture. After looking in that one, we'd rub twice as hard trying to erase them, at times plastering pure manure on our faces, minus the dew.

After the eleventh day we lost all interest in the old woman. At first we thought of going to her house and plastering her face with cow manure for ten days, but instead we kept clear of her, and as far as we were concerned she could get her own coal or freeze. We decided she must be in cahoots with the cows to procure entertainment for them throughout the summer, and we heard later that during those ten days three cows had died. The autopsy probably revealed they had died laughing.

As the sun got warmer that summer, we were blanketed with our little unwanted friends. You could almost see them settling themselves in for an indefinite stay. We couldn't figure out where they found the room, but satisfied our curiosity by saying we must have grown some more face. If someone else had told us of a cure, we would have found it hard to say no, but it was a subject we tried to evade, and we resigned ourselves to the fact we were destined to be human freckles forever.

One day a friend of mine traded me his pocket watch and chain for a ring I had found on the shore. This watch wasn't very reliable, except when you dipped it at a right angle. How proud I was on the way to school this day. The chain with links as big as quarters bent me to a stooped position and dangled from a button on my pants, with the watch in my vest pocket. Fifteen minutes before school took in, I was flattered to have two really good-looking girls ask me the time of day. I was so excited I nearly ripped my vest apart getting the watch out. Holding tightly to the chain and acting experienced while the girls were waiting to hear the time , a bully piped up and said, "Holy Cripes, he's even got freckles on his watch."

We had to live with these freckles for many years and we knew it was something we couldn't hide. We were able to relax one day a year, on Halloween. We didn't even need a mask.

Please Miss, We Found The Mouse In Benny's Sweater
Freckles or not we still had to attend school. I clearly remember the first day Murray and I entered the big red brick building. What we thought was a huge dining room (we were delighted thinking they were just going to feed us each day, then send us home), soon turned out to be our school room. It was lined with five rows of double desks, each row allowing a four-foot aisle for lining up pupils in double file to march out of the room.

In those days they never registered the children months ahead like they do now. We just paraded in, with the teacher not even knowing we existed, let alone our names. Ninety per cent of us had never been any farther from home than the outhouse, ours only thirty-seven feet from the house and there wasn't too much of interest there. The first hour was quite exciting as we moved our heads constantly, looking at the pencil sharpener, the teacher's desk, the shades with strings on them, and the little chains on the pull-in windows, the likes of which we'd never seen before. But after about two hours of this sitting, we began to get terribly lonesome for Ma or anyone in the family, except Pa, although I must admit Pa's actions kept us from getting bored. Murray and I seated together were supposed to line up in separate aisles to go home. Instead Murray, glued to me as if we were Siamese twins, slid over into my aisle, leaving one small pupil to walk out alone.

About sixty pupils attended the first day, and our teacher was a kind-hearted woman who knew how to contend with lonesome, little, first-time-away-from-home greenhorns. Murray and I even today have never been ones to be last in line, so we wiggled our way to the very front seat, thinking if there was anything to be handed out, even if it was more freckles, we wouldn't miss out. Not too long after this we found we had made a mistake, as we were very noticeable to the teacher. It was the same as standing right up at the pulpit with the minister. We could be seen from every angle.

The first morning we wore the same new clothes, ribbed black stockings, with outstanding ribs, gum rubbers and pants held up by two-inch wide police braces, like a hockey player. I think there must have been a cheap sale of red sweater coats before school opened, as all the boys plus a few girls had them on. I think the teacher and the principal had them on too.

The teacher went up and down the aisle with a notepad taking the name of each kid and we wished she'd say to us, "I'm sorry, freckle-faced fellows aren't allowed in this school. Go home at once." When she came to Murray and I, she gently asked Murray his name first. He gave a mournful sigh and poured out his full name. She asked me mine, and after I gave her mine, also including my middle name, she asked if we were cousins, only to get fast double answers that we were brothers. "Which one is the oldest?" she asked. I looked her in the eye and in a bored voice, as if she'd asked me if we lived in the same town, said, "Please Miss, I'm the oldest." "How old are you Andy?" Hearing the answer since I was two, I was getting disgusted with the whole business, and replied in monotone, "Please Miss, I'm twenty minutes older than him." This made the teacher chuckle a little, as she only then realized we were twins. We then thought she might be passing out gifts for twins, like maybe some chocolate-flavoured freckle remover, but no dice.

It wasn't long before the teacher began studying the good and bad sitters, as she began shifting Mary with Agnes, and John with Charlie. The penalty for the talkers was to sit right up front where she could keep an eye on them . . . our aim was to be perfectly good, no talking, and then she'd put us in the back, so we could talk our hearts out, as up till now there was nothing given out, except slurs now and then, when we deserved them. After awhile we were the quietest kids in the outfit, sitting listless, like sick zombies. Then came our promotion to the rear. Taking our belongings, Murray carried our reader, and filled with pride and bursting with things to say and do, I trailed behind with our school bag. We couldn't have been placed in a better spot, second seat from the back. Now we had two red-sweatered kids in front of us and another two behind. The yearning for Ma was decreasing and we were able to take a good look at the objects in the back of the room—radiators and pictures that we were unable to see when we occupied the front seat, also we were closer to the door we walked through when school was dismissed.

A buddy in front of us who had on one of those bulky red sweaters had a chewed wad of about five sticks of gum stuck right in the centre on the back of his sweater, which looked like a big grey spider in a red web. I'll never know how it got there unless his mother stuck it there to hold his sweater together. It was knotted in around the wool, and how Murray and I struggled, taking turns trying to get that gum out! The owner of the chaw was accepting our grabbing as if he were a small puppy, and we were gently stroking him. The teacher had been drilling us for hours that no one was to turn around in their seats, even if there was a man from outer space sitting on the radiator (who, by the way, might have been wearing one of those red sweater coats), and it was for that reason Benny kept perfectly still while we tugged violently to unravel something we thought shouldn't be there. We worked under strain trying to keep an eye on the teacher. Finally the woolen fibres could take no more and the gum ball was yanked out, leaving quite a scar on Benny's sweater, as though he'd been shot with a bazooka. The wad with the red wool clinging to it now resembled a small mouse that had just had a dye job.

The fun started when Murray and I made a game out of it. We'd shoot it from the bottom of the desk and try to make a basket by having it go in the inkwell at the top. It was a miracle to get it in the first shot. Trying again and again, one time Murray slapped the wooly object too hard and it landed near the teacher's feet. She gave a shrill shriek and jumped back with her hands over her head, as though we had pointed a gun at her.

"Where did you get the mouse?" she screamed. "Please Miss, we found it in Benny's sweater." Benny of course stared straight ahead, not daring to turn around, yet wondering if he should get a lawyer to argue the point. The teacher ordered me to pick up the well-clothed hunk of chewing gum and put it in the wastebasket at the side of her desk, even though we wanted to take it home with us for a pet.

That was the end of our back seat affair, and we'd just moved in. The teacher began talking to two girls in front seats. We saw them gather up their belongings and walk toward us with astonished looks on their faces. Then the sweet voice floats back to us from the front of the room, "Murray and Andy, bring your things and sit up front." Benny had a sad look on his face as though he was sorry to see us go—the two who had nearly torn his sweater to shreds, and accused him of harbouring a mouse in his sweater.

The Case Of The Missing Strap

Then we graded into this crummy teacher's classroom. I often thought of her as Pa's double; they had a lot in common.

Over Miss Brindell's desk hung a picture of the Quebec bridge. Many times I and others gazed seriously at it, as it was directly over the teacher's desk; and when the answer to a question was rather hard, where else would you look but straight ahead, wishing for the picture to fall off the wall and knock her unconscious? But no such luck. Murray and I, keeping the strap in motion this season, had hands that were swollen like raised bread dough. One day we decided to stay in at recess to catch up on some of our work. At least that's what we let the teacher think. She was out of the room so we had full control. Our aim was to do away with the strap if we had to chew it up and swallow it. Murray slipped to her desk, and knowing by heart it was in the second drawer, he seized it, wishing he could use it on Miss Brindell before we hid it.

We had only minutes to decide what to do with it, as the rest of the class and teacher would be in the room soon. The two-foot square picture of the Quebec Bridge looming above her desk was a perfect place for the strap, which was only a foot long. My first toss centered it perfectly behind the picture.

A half hour of class time went by—quite a long time for Miss Brindell to abstain from using the strap. At last Murray and I were the culprits again, as Murray was caught whispering to me not to look toward the picture above her desk.

Rolling up her sleeves, our sweet teacher pulled out the second drawer in her desk. Her first reach was useless, and she took out the register of names to look underneath. Red with rage she renewed her hunt, shouting, "Has anyone seen the strap?" This was answered immediately by everyone in the class, except Murray and me. "No Miss." Our heads are lowered and we avoid looking at each other, also the picture. "I want everyone to clear everything out of their desks to see if the strap is there."

It never took Murray and I long to comply with her order, as we only had a small slate, a coverless geography book, and an old sandwich that was a lovely shade of green, beginning to get hard and scratchy on the corners which we should have offered Miss Brindell for her lunch.

Picking a favourite pupil, she said, "Mary, please go to Miss Walsh's room and see if she got the loan of it." But her pet came back saying, "No, she doesn't have it."

For days, weeks, months the search went on. It was the first time Murray and I had the full use of our fingers on both hands. There were rumours that Miss Brindell was going to bring in some Pinkerton security men to find the strap.

After three months of the lost strap, our hands were beginning to look sort of feminine and sexy.

As the urgency of strap searching wore off Murray and I were beginning to get a little lax, and were almost to the point of throwing a spitball at the teacher. One day a fellow pupil who lived close to the teacher began talking about the teacher losing the strap. At the same time he was fiddling in a small candy bag popping colourful jelly beans and chocolates in his mouth. He had no thoughts of offering us one, even though we were slobbering at the sight of them. Murray said to him, "If you give us a candy each we'll tell you where the strap is hidden, provided you don't tell the teacher." (If we had had it, we would have told him the route to Captain Kidd's treasure chest.) At once he gave us a honeymoon, chocolate-coated candy, and we divulged the hiding place behind the Bridge while he gave us a secret-partner look saying, "Mum's the word."

Next day as usual, Murray and I were taking chances talking about homework unfinished knowing the strap wasn't around, even though we had a few bruises on our knuckles from the pointer, her weapon during the strap's absence. Finally we were caught fooling around with a rubber ball and were told to come forward. We prepared to accept the pointer.

With it she gave you only two belts. We could stand that. But, like in the song "Amazing Grace, " what was lost had now been found and we were astounded to see her reach over and open the second drawer to withdraw the killer strap. (If only Amazing Grace could have stepped in to save us.) Ten stinging wallops on each dainty pinky was quickly followed by ten more, the latter for hiding the strap.

After school that afternoon we waited for our friend, who also happened to be the teacher's neighbour, and probably a Pinkerton agent in disguise. We got him in an alley. Warning him not to tell the teacher about the whipping we gave him was the same as telling him about the strap, because it was only minutes before Murray and I appeared before Mrs. Brindell again who held the strap dangling from her hand, like a cow's tail, and our loaves of bread began rising again. We knew that if we ever snitched the strap again, we'd never hide it behind that picture of the Quebec bridge. We'd have thrown it under the real one.

The Corpseless Wake And The Salmon Sandwiches
A surefire way of having a day off from school was if someone in the school died.

Although Pa seemed hardhearted at times, if any sickness or accident befell our school chums or their parents he showed much sympathy.

In small towns when shocking news came, it was a good feeling. Not that we liked to see the death or accident occur, but the fast relaying of the news to people who had never heard it made the messenger feel important watching the face of the listener.

This day the news was carried by Murray, (a great one to expand small stories) as he came home from school. We lived almost two miles from school, and because Murray knew the victim, he thought of him over and over again all the way home. And not being at the scene of the accident, Murray enlarged it to a high degree. The many different tales of this poor kid's death were enough to make parents lock their kids in the house forever.

Murray's lips were moving a mile a minute, trying to tell Pa the gruelling story in one breath. I knew the victim as well as Murray, but Pa never suspected I did during this terrible tale. After noticing the closest one of Pa's eyes to me teared up, my eye closest to him moistened up a little too. Murray's big eyes had no time to leak up as he was still putting in things that must have happened now that he had Pa in such a sad trance.

With a solemn look in Pa's direction, I said, "There'll be no school tomorrow." Then I used the example of the time the girl died in our class a year ago and there had been no school until after she was buried. Pa nodded in total sympathy.

The victim was a kid our age who had been run over by a lumber truck and killed instantly—so Murray had heard. The embellishments to this were too gory to relate here. Pa knew his mother and father, and of course that well-known sentence that's spoken at times like this popped out of me, "He was such a nice fellow." Although we didn't tell Pa, I had had a glorious, bare-knuckled fist fight with him about two weeks before, because he had beat me in a marble game and I wouldn't surrender the marbles I owed him. He won the fight with a left to my teeth and loosened up the whitest tooth I owned. I would have gladly run him over with a five-hundred-pound roller. But now that he was dead, and feeling joyful that there was no school, I too could afford to sadden up tightly. "Well," says Pa, "you fellows will have to go see him, as in a few days he'll be buried. Don't forget to bring something." I told Pa I'd be bringing Murray, but Pa meant food, as was the custom in those days.

We couldn't bring a cake, as Ma never had one ready; the co-op store was closed, and we were short on eggs. Running over to the small corner store with fifteen cents, we bought a can of salmon for Ma to make sandwiches, and that was to be our presentation in respect.

A dozen or more sandwiches were thrown together and done up in the wax paper that had held a bar of shortening. We were proud mourners leaving our house on a Tuesday night, with our Sunday suits on, well versed in changing a smile in seconds to complete regret. Murray carried the vitals, while I carried the sombre looks.

Nearing the house, Murray and I were astonished there was no big crowd, or at least a car stopped near his house. Well we thought, cars were scarce around Sydney Mines. Surely there would be some for the funeral.

The house was in darkness except for a weak light burning in a small room. Rapping on the door, not too loud, so as not to arouse the corpse, we knocked a second time. With the sandwiches held to our chest like a bridal wreath, we could make out the outline of a young man in the dimly-lit room, and our eyes followed his shadow as he came to greet us.

The dead boy opened the door. Too numb to run, and speechless, Murray passed him the sandwiches. Then with hardly any breath left in his body he said, "We thought you were dead." The deceased went into a fit of laughter, saying, "That makes four people who thought I got run over by a lumber truck." And added,

"Come in." Quite disappointed at this news we entered the small house, and still in a spooky mood thinking he had probably just gotten up from his coffin to answer the door when we had rapped twice.

All the sorriness was leaving me as I thought, "He took all my marbles, and besides that my tooth is still loose." But I couldn't get the nerve to take a sneaky poke at him because I felt he had some hypnotic wave about him that would destroy me in seconds. So I allowed the fight I'd had with him to leave my brain and attended to the business of his wake, which was why we were there in the first place.

We stayed only a few minutes after we went inside when we found out he wasn't climbing back into his final resting place. He told us he nearly got run over, but the guy driving swerved into the ditch and missed him by inches.

What were we to tell Pa, after all the sadness we had bestowed upon him? Why Murray and I had declared it a legal holiday from school to mourn, and Pa didn't eat his porridge that morning, and had even forgot his chewing tobacco for the mine.

The live corpse would have to commit suicide in front of us, so Murray wouldn't be accused of exaggerating. Murray and I took sneaky glances at each other just as the kid went into another fit of laughter, as though he was playing a ghost prank on us. Our eyes searched for his coffin. We never stayed long, expecting that he'd take a terrible laughing spell again and retire to his resting box. Were we to take our sandwiches when we left? When we entered, he had accepted them, and placed them on the pantry table with ease. Standing in a run position, Murray and I wished him health as Murray picked up the sandwiches and flew to the same door that the living dead had ushered us through. Looking back, we said goodnight as we walked frantically past his house. We never did much talking until we got about two blocks from the haunted abode. Then under a street light in town, with living people passing by, Murray and I tested the sandwiches. We didn't want to test too many, as Ma knew she'd made an even dozen.

Passing through town with the wreath of sandwiches tucked next to Murray's chest, we headed for home. Although darkness had set in for an hour or so, Pa was still in the old rocker with a grey look of sadness on his face, while Ma was emptying the grounds from the old teapot in the sink. As was our habit, we peeked in the window first, seeing Pa, and knew sadness pervaded the kitchen for the young kid, who was in better shape than Murray and I. Murray had just gotten over scarlet fever, and I was having trouble with a cavity in a back tooth.

We'd have to go in, as it looked as though Pa was going to stay up all night to hear the details. (I guess Murray took after him in that respect.) Into the house we flowed, with Murray putting the ten sandwiches on the table next to Pa. "Why didn't you leave the sandwiches?" Pa yelled, as Murray and I sported our Sunday clothes past Pa without inspection. Murray straightens up stiffly, and looks at Pa, "The kid wasn't dead, he answered the door." I could see Pa twitch a couple of times, as though he thought he was dreaming, and Ma opened up the sandwiches. Had we been a family to play pranks on Pa, he would have chuckled heartily at this news, but no, he plummeted from his chair, looking at the clock saying, "I should have been in bed two hours ago." Pa's expression had changed from remorse to relief, and he spidered his way to bed.

Ma, Murray and I had a light snack before retiring—

something different for a change—salmon sandwiches, and I thought the kid could have at least given me back my marbles as I had attended his wake and all. I guess the only way we were going to get a school holiday out of this guy was if we got the mafia to take out a contract on him.

Ice Cream Gravel

Another big excuse for no school was summer holidays. If they had ever decided to have school throughout the summer months, we would have formed a vigilante group to push the school over the cliff.

During the hot summer months, free from school, it was pure joy to see the huge billboard advertising a strawberry ice cream cone. The cone was about six feet high, the top overflowing with pink ice cream and huge chunks of strawberries peeking out. It would have been great to be a termite. We could have devoured the sign in no time. As it was it took a lot of self control to keep from tearing off the paper ice cream cone and eating it there and then.

In the spring we'd wait for those large erectors to scrape off the old ad, praying they would put the new ice cream picture up right away, so we could drool over it. Sitting there on the dampened grass we'd watch them as they mixed their concoction of what looked like flour and water. We would even have had a lick at that. Then they'd take their long-handled brushes and run them over the twelve-by-twenty-four sign, letting the paste set for a few minutes before rolling the colourful paper across the board from one end to the other. Soon the bright lettering of *Brookfield Ice Cream, A Dream of Fruit and Cream* could be seen from quite a distance. Not long afterward the cone came into view and that's what we had been waiting for. It was new, clean and bright, and our mouths watered, knowing that as big as it was anyone of us could have eaten every bite of it without waste. We'd stay there for hours after it was put up, dreaming and wondering how we could get a nickel to stop the gnawing in our stomachs.

It was Pa's custom to buy us a cone if we graded, and that was quite a gamble as the marks we were bringing home didn't look as though we'd have any taste buds left for this scrumptuous stuff. But things evened up pretty good. Out of the four of us, there would usually be two that made the grade, Billy and Murray, which left Teedy and I tormenting the winning brothers for a bite or three of theirs, or even the pleasure of watching them eat it.

One year we each had three ice cream cones (mine was maple, my favourite). It was the year we all graded, as big an event as the Queen's Jubilee. Then a close friend of Pa's treated us to one and the third one was given to us by the preacher, who made frequent calls. (Probably feeling that of all his flock, we were the ones needing the most surveillance, and that if he could fatten us up it would be harder for us to get around and into trouble.) That was one summer we didn't stare too long at the big cone on the side of the road.

It was always Murray who was picked by Pa to go and get the ice cream cones from the store an eighth of a mile from home. We couldn't understand why, except that he was quicker on the run, which accounted for his nickname, Monkey, which he despised and which always sent him into a rage. (Pa would never allow four of us to go together. Maybe he thought we'd abscond with all that money.) But whatever happened to Murray on those trips to the store for the ice cream, we'll never know. Where the weather was a little warm, we gave him the benefit of the doubt and allowed the shrinkage and settling of the ice cream which took place from the store to home to the heat.

One time on his swift marathon, racing along the small gravel path from the store, a painful, stone-stubbing big toe made him fall to the ground, decapitating the cones. The blobs of ice cream landed in the gravel, leaving Murray tightly gripping the four empty cones. He wasted no time looking at his two skinned arms, or the hurt toe, but as fast as he splashed down into the pebbled path, he snatched the ice cream off the warm stones and squashed it down into the cone so quickly he looked like one of those guys on the Keystone Cops. The running, falling, picking up and plopping back into the cone were done in one swift motion. According to Murray this was what happened, and that accounted for the shape of the ice cream. We weren't too concerned about his falling even if he tripped over the cliff as long as we ended up eating the ice cream. No wonder we gave him such a disgusted sneer when he'd pass us a shrunk-up ice cream in a wet cone. How could this happen every time? or could it have been his tongue with a little gravel sprinkled on to make his story believable. However there was no use arguing with him, as at least we were grasping the cone, and would greedily take a big lick of the ice cream coming up with more gravel than ice cream. This slowed us down considerably, but made the ice cream last longer. We even made it musical by sputtering the gravel out in an old tin pan, in rhythmic fashion. Pa never knew about our gravelly ice cream cones. He'd have told us not to eat them. And we knew we'd never get another nickel out of him to buy one. So we spent our younger years eating at least one gravelly ice cream a year, which leads me to believe this may have been the cause for Teedy and I having to have operations for kidney stones.

Twin Werewolves

Murray's swiftness was known throughout the neighbourhood, and one Halloween it really paid off. A group of us was lined up against a stone wall checking our loot, when a car rolled toward us with its lights off. With no time for us to run, six policemen stepped out and marched along beside us as if we were under an army inspection. Each of our faces was studied by the police. All at once three of them grabbed Murray, lifted him off his feet, and dragged him toward their car. After this move the rest of us flew into the darkness, wondering what was to become of Murray. They must have wanted the Halloween treats he had in his old pillow case.

I raced home and jumped into bed figuring that the safest place to be. Waiting there, fully clothed, under the covers, I thought of all kinds of things that might have happened to Murray. Then I heard someone moving. The jig was up. A policeman must have been hiding there to nab me. Stealthily, someone climbed down from the attic. Suffocating under the covers, I could sense the policeman's gun aimed at me. I kept very still for a few minutes, wondering when they were going to make their arrest, and if I should get Pa as my lawyer (fat chance). I could see the courtroom. The judge was Pa, so was the prosecuting attorney, and each of the jurors. I could hear Pa's courtroom rumble, "Just look at this boy who has committed the vile, unpardonable sin of standing against a stone wall, the same boy who does no lessons, skips school, and will not wash behind his left ear. Yes, here we have

Andy Macdonald, charged with the odious crime of standing against a stone wall on Halloween. We will find him guilty, and he will be hanged by the neck until dead." Then cries of "Bring on the executioner"— who happens to be none other than Pa, with Miss Brindell tying the noose knot.

Slowly I slipped back to reality. The policeman wasn't making his move for some reason. It was then I figured it must be Pa with his sabre, waiting there to run me through for my criminal act—not wanting the shame of a jury trial.

Quietly and oh so slowly, I pulled the covers back so that just a third of one eye was peering out. Expecting a bayonet to the eyeball at any second, I scanned the darkness, and just had time to see a wiry form leaping at me out of the corner. I now knew this was no policeman, this was no Pa—this was some escaped lunatic, or quite possibly a werewolf.

Threshing and wrestling the ghoul around on the bed all tangled up in the covers, I thought I recognized the gruntings and mutterings of this crazed beast. I whispered faintly, "Murray."

"Yeah, oh it's you Andy, thank God. I thought you were a policeman hiding under the covers."

"That's nothing Murray, I thought you were a werewolf."

Murray said that he had sprung out of the policemen's clutches while they were opening the car door for him to enter. Away he had gone down the road, in the same direction as the police car. Hot on his heels in the car, the police said later, they had never known a human could run that fast. After about a mile down the road, Murray cut through a field toward home, and the police gave up the chase.

Whispering very low in case Pa was in the picture, Murray told me that he had passed two lovers sitting

32

on a tree stump, who shouted something about a small tornado passing them. A few days afterwards, one of the policeman cornered us, saying he was sorry for the mistake that night. We told him to think nothing of it. It had caused us no problems, except that we both ended up in a scuffle with a werewolf, twin werewolves to be exact. They had been looking for someone who looked like Murray. He said they had had their Buick to the floor, but couldn't get within twenty feet of him. They wondered if Murray was equipped with a hidden motor.

Fertilizer Fantasy
But the wrestle with the werewolf was nothing compared to when Murray and I had to tackle one hundred pounds of fertilizer, and a seventy-five pound bag of seed potatoes.

During the depression, free seed and fertilizer was metered out to the needy and underprivileged, so that everyone could have his own little garden. It was called Victory Gardens.

Trying to conserve his small paycheque, Pa heard this good news at a card game, and we twins were hand-picked for the job. (I guess Pa figured we came as a set, and we were to remain as a set, even when we went to the toilet.)

The big problem was how to transport them from the station. Pa never worried about this. Once he gave us the orders, it was up to us to get the stuff home, even if we had to push the potatoes along one by one with our noses. Murray and I scurried around that night and found a wheel off an old wheelbarrow, and I convinced Murray that we could rig up some sort of a vehicle next day, saying the wheel was the most important part and we already had that.

The deadline was next day at eight-thirty a.m., so

we set the Big Ben for four a.m., as we were as bad as Pa and never wanted to miss anything gratis. When the alarm rang we shot out of bed, dressed and ate a sandwich, then began hammering and pounding like blacksmiths. This went on for hours, right down to the handles, knowing that we needed at least half an hour to get to the station. Our potato conveyance was built in one flat piece, like a floor, with no sides. We had a good start on a house, and used as many nails as Pa had building ours. At first we fought over who was going to shove it, but didn't put up much of a rumpus after finding out how hard it was to push. Have you ever tried pushing a house on one wheel?

It was quite wobbly and off-centre, and when we first reached the railroad station we were a little em-barassed and wished we had worn masks. We were confronted with half-ton trucks, and small cars with their trunks open. Murray and I slipped inconspi-ciously into line and proceeded to the huge freight car manned by two CNR officials. We knew our wagon couldn't stand the four-foot drop of weight from the train car without disintegrating. It would be like drop-ping the moon onto a card table. So we convinced the men to drop our sack of potatoes and fertilizer on the ground. We should have asked them to haul our share to our house on the train. Trouble started when Mur-ray and I tried to heave the potatoes and fertilizer out of the way, so others could receive theirs.

Really holding up proceedings, and almost rupturing ourselves struggling and wrestling with the fertilizer, we felt like two of the seven dwarfs attempting to carry off the wicked queen's castle, with all the King's men waiting in line to kill us.

The potatoes weren't nearly as heavy. I could have balanced them on my head. We figured the thing to do first was to try to heave the fertilizer aboard the legless wagon. It took us an hour to do that, and every ounce of our strength. It was the first time I ever heard a wagon grunt, as the fertilizer alone was an overload by at least one hundred pounds. However, we weren't under any circumstances going to leave the potatoes, or Pa would have rounded up a posse to attack the train. We would have eaten them right there, so as not to waste them. Rather than trying to drag them for two miles, we undertook the job of hassling them on with the fertilizer. Groaning and straining like ants lifting a brick onto a dinky toy, the wheel flopped off our wheelbarrow.

The day was getting on, and we were still only about fifty feet from where we had received them. Pa would think we had walked to Idaho for the potatoes. Running across the street, I borrowed a hammer and we nailed on the wheel. With me holding the sacks and Murray hefting the handles we managed another hundred feet, until the wheel left its rightful place again. With luck we'd be home by Christmas, and Santa could help us plant them in the snow. I trudged along to the nearest house and again got a hammer. After a few wacks and whams, the wheel felt taut. It was now my turn to grasp the weak handles, and maneuver the load toward home. We were surprised when we advanced a quarter of a mile or more without mishap. Then having wheel trouble again, we employed without pay two ladies in their seventies to grab a corner of the sacks and lift, so Murray could steer the wheel on.

Better than a mile to go, we were now two hours on the hike, I thought if Murray could pull over to the grassy part of the highway, I could drag the potatoes along the grass, and lighten his load considerably.

Sweating and grunting furiously he aimed his steer to the grassy section. No trouble for me to roll the potatoes off. They looked comfortable on the ground, as though asleep. With a good grip on one of the ears of the bag, I received new strength and continued on without struggle. Murray looked relieved and also seemed to be gaining a few knots per hour. Craning my neck backwards, I found why my pull was getting lighter. A long row of shiny seed potatoes strung out behind me. My potato sack couldn't take the friction anymore, and had spilled the potatoes out one by one, ready for planting there on the highway. We wore large loose-fitting jackets in the spring, so I hollered to Murray to come back. I filled every one of his pockets, then tucked his jacket into his pants, and filled his jacket front and back. When I had finished sculpting him, he looked like a muscle-bound midget covered with tumours. I filled my attire with the remainder and off we waddled—two miniature Charles Atlases, hoping nobody we knew would see us. The condition we were in, we should have been taken home by ambulance. Any part of our body that was itchy had to go unscratched as it's impossible to touch your flesh through potatoes.

With half a mile to go, Murray is still wheeling, and is not as flexible as before the torn potato bag. He is potato laden. With the upper part of my torso bulging, I grab the potatoes from Murray's bulging pockets and aim them for the torn bag, and holding together the hole and the top of the bag, I throw them over my shoulder. On we go to our square red house, knowing Pa will be in the window, wondering if we have run away from home. After our early morning departure, we arrive in the late afternoon, and head for the old shed to evict our load.

Pa puts a small barrel in front of us to deposit the potatoes from our grotesque forms. Nothing is lost, and now we have too much help from Pa, Teedy and Billy, who carry the fertilizer from the weary wagon to the shed.

Back in the house happiness adorns each face. There is even a reluctant smile from Pa, which is his show of appreciation when we get something for nothing.

That spring the sun was generous and there wasn't much rain, so our land was ready for early planting. Our fifty-by-fifty garden plot was soon smothered with fertilizer. Pa bought a few packages of beets, peas, beans and raddish, but the seed potatoes are carried to the small cellar to be eaten. Every seed is planted, and the two-week wait is on. In two weeks nothing is peeping through. After the third week a crippled bean springs up with only one wing. It gets so much attention from us that it slowly gets rusty, and dies. The land looks rich, but not even a weed ventures near.

It now dawns on us that Pa has used too much fertilizer, and has burnt the seeds to a crisp before they even germinated. The seed potatoes are snuggled safely in the cellar. Thank God we didn't plant them.

Pa, of course, doesn't take the blame for cremating the seeds. He manages to push the blame onto Murray and I, saying we must have picked a bad batch of fertilizer. Had the fertilizer been edible, it never would have been used on the small garden, and Pa's few seeds would have at least popped up for a day or two.

We were lucky to have any land left, as after the fertilizer Pa dumped on, it's a wonder it didn't eat off half the cliff. By the end of the summer, our little wooden fence which surrounded our small garden, although new before planting, was now honeycombed at the bottom as if soaked in a strong acid. Finally the small fence could take no more and keeled over onto the plantless garden. So much for free victory fertilizer!

Chapter Two

We Loved The Sabbath So

We Lived At Church

Sunday school (I shudder at the name even today) was at two p.m. If it had been at two a.m., Pa would have expected us to be at our best even at that hour. My first recollection of Sunday school was one Christmas when I was about four. I had a piece to memorize for the concert and everyone in the house was after me about it; so by the time the concert rolled around I could almost say it backwards.

I only wished I had said it backwards, because with the qualms I went through to say that verse, you'd have thought I was a ballerina on top of a music box. The worst thing they did was place me next to the M.C. He gave me the first line, which in my panic had slid right out of my mind. It was quite an undertaking to perform in front of a live audience. The only natural thing to do was grab hold of the M.C.'s baggy pant leg.

I was to recite the first and last verse of "The Night before Christmas". I didn't walk off with a prize but almost walked off with the M.C.'s pants. Had I recited the whole poem, the M.C. would have had to be taken off in a strait jacket to the nearest mental institution, because as soon as he gave the first line I started pulling on his pant leg, and before my lines were finished I had almost yanked his pants right off. I was hellbent on clutching his pants as that was all that was keeping me from collapsing. With a grip on his right pant leg, I was under his legs, at times making a complete circle, but still holding on to his pants. I never looked at the audience at all, just kept staring straight up into the M.C.'s eyes, as if he was Romeo and I was Juliet. When he heard me mutter "and to all a goodnight", he mumbled, "Thank God, he's finished." I got many requests to go to Hollywood after this, but rejected them all as I heard no one there had loose pants like the Sunday school M.C.

This was my first remembrance of Sunday school and my love of it lessened with every passing week over the years.

Saturdays were wonderful. We were free to run and play. But on Sundays we were imprisoned with Pa. We'd have preferred a lion. A staunch Presbyterian, we were supposed to follow suit; but he didn't know we used another suit. We four brothers dreaded Sunday because the itinerary was as follows: Up early Sunday after a late Saturday night, then a bath in a galvanized wash tub. Our breakfast of beans was eaten very quietly. We all made sure our throats were cleared of frogs (we usually left them out in the porch to hop around, until we were ready for church) before sitting down with Pa. It was like eating breakfast with the King. His Majesty sat at the head of the table and there never was a great rush to sit beside him, unless you were positively sure that the ear next to him was shining with cleanliness, and polished with a chamois. But if you gave that ear an extra good washing, ten to one he would ask you to show him the other one.

It seemed that no matter how long we took to clean our ears, Pa would find a foreign object that had evaded the washrag. There were one or two sets of earmuffs we used in the winter, but we decided if we wore them in the summer when the temperature was in the low eighties, we'd just be coaxing Pa to investigate.

We thought of getting one of those false ears they wear at Halloween, so we could have slipped it on when he asked to see the other ear. And every word addressed to his Highness had to have "Sir" after it. We felt like four little privates, with dazzling white ears.

Our four small suits were hung in a very orderly fashion upstairs. It seemed as though you'd turn into a distinguished actor and become very stiff as soon as you put the coat on, as though rigor mortis was setting in. I now believe the coat was too tight, as I never was too supple in any of the four suits I owned in eighteen years. I often felt if I could have thrown myself around on the floor for a few minutes, do a few cartwheels and somersaults, it would have loosened my attire considerably, but Pa would have had me deported to a contortionist colony. I suppose I could have told him I was taking a fit, except I don't think you're able to stop in the middle of a fit to tell people you are taking one.

Ma would help us dress after breakfast, and each of us would check the other knowing the prone parts Pa would look for. He might find a small hole in the heel of a sock, a wrong-buttoned shirt, or a freckle out of place. These would somehow pass Ma's inspection, but errors like these were met with heavy sentencing from Pa.

Attending church with Pa was horrible. In fact anything with Pa around was fiendish, like having Frankenstein for a constant companion. The walk to church was a mile, but seemed like ten, striding beside Pa, dressed to the hilt, but stiff as a sword. On our way, we'd sort of trail behind, not so far that Pa couldn't hear our footsteps, just far enough so he couldn't hear us deciding whose turn it was to sit beside him during the service. We never ever middled Pa. It only took one to suffer sitting beside him, and the rest of us would sit by the one seated next to Pa, silently wishing we had thirty more kids in our family so we could sit across the aisle from Pa. We would have loved to sit behind him (like maybe out on the step) but we knew that would never happen, unless he grew two eyes on the nape of his neck. Teedy usually ended up next to Pa, certainly not for the love of him, but because we forced him in a nice way, by pushing his pudgy little body against Pa. He couldn't put up much of a fuss with Pa looking on. Pa might ask him what he was fussing about, and if Teedy told him the truth he would have had to sit on Pa's lap, leaving one of us to absorb the heat from Pa's leg.

There was one hymn book between the five of us, and you-know-who held it. Teedy, the closest to Pa, held the other half, and should have been born with an extension on his arm. That was just another punishment you had to endure when you sat next to Pa. Teedy would either have to stand on tiptoe or drag Pa down to his level, book and all, which he tried once, but all he succeeded in doing was pressing very hard on the page, until it left its binding and floated downward through the air, in flying carpet style, to settle peacefully on the toe caps of Pa's high black boots.

The reaching and trying to keep in height with Pa was bad enough, but your stiff suit would only allow you to reach so far, and then your hand would tremble as though you had started to freeze to death. A relieved look would gleam on Teedy's fat jaws when the minister would say, "We'll just sing the first and second stanza of this hymn." I think he took pity on Teedy's strained position, also he didn't want any more hymn books destroyed. We could notice the preacher on a bending slant unconsciously trying to help Teedy keep his equilibrium as Pa blasted out the hymn.

Pa's Pains

One Sunday one of us heard Pa complaining about his bowels. He was talking to Ma, and we acted as though we weren't interested. But we absorbed every word because we thought he wouldn't go to church, and we'd have a ball with Pa home waiting for the concoction of cream of tartar and soda Ma had fixed for him that morning to bulldoze a clearing through his large intestine. But Pa continued getting dressed, and our spirits sunk. He might surrender, we thought, before eleven a.m. as it was now ten-thirty a.m. I guess he analyzed the happy looks we four had on and that prompted him to go.

Pa was kind of mad at us on the way to church as we all gave up looking him in the eye when he spoke to us. Hearing his symptoms all morning, our eyes focused on his hind parts.

After a half an hour of the preacher expounding on the terrible suffering of Job, Pa's belly gurgled, and we thought this a normal sound as there were times when ours would make a similar sound. Only difference was ours was a lonesome feeling for Ma, as it seemed like ages on Sundays since we had had a good talk with Ma, we were on the go so much. Before the preacher came to an end, Pa stood up, holding on to the back of the front seat. Working his way through our dangling feet, he proceeded toward the back of the church, amidst turning heads and whispers. After we studied this quick action of Pa's, him being well in the lead, there was nothing for his small military contingency to do but follow the leader. Directly out back into the washroom we marched after Pa, while the good preacher was still deep in Job's trials and tribulations. When we arrived at the scene, no Pa. Then in a small compartment, with the door fully locked against on-lookers, a voice was saying in a grunting tone, "In the name of heavens, you never followed me out here!" The crisp voice of Pa gave us the impression we were to go back to our seats, but when he heard us take a complete wheel to head back into church, he weakly squeaked, "Wait for me." Then he led us out into the morning sunshine, one half hour before that interesting subject, the morning benediction, was due. Later, when a member of the congregation asked us why Pa and we four walked out of church a half hour early, we told them Pa was so affected by the tale of Job's suffering he just couldn't bear to hear anymore of it and we all had to go along to comfort him.

I'm sure the minister at those services worked long and hard to find a sermon lengthy enough to torture us to death. Singing was the only thing that kept us alert, and once the organist slipped from her stool to sit on a chair for the main sermon, we'd think, "Oh no, can we stand it?" Then we'd brace our feet, hide behind another brother from Pa, and have a well-observed nap. We often practiced trying to keep our eyes open while we slept, like fish, but it never worked. Sometimes a hard stare from Pa, when your eyes connected, was a good wake-up signal. I had heard so much about Jonah and the whale, I was beginning to know the man intimately, and as for the whale, why couldn't he swallow Pa just before church, then throw him up after church?

The benediction was a godsend; and we'd listen attentively, knowing that that was the end, and short and sweet it was to our ears. We used to envy the kids whose fathers stayed at home, and sent them to church alone. But in a way, it was a good thing Pa escorted us, because without a chaperone, we'd probably be the only kids in the world ever to attack a preacher at the pulpit.

Billy On His Belly

One day when Pa couldn't make it, the minister almost threw us out of the church, and it was all Billy's fault. Billy was always the sportiest one in the family, even though three-quarters of his apparel belonged to an older brother, Freddy (the remaining quarter to Pearl). Nevertheless he had a good build, and carried himself well, and his outside clothes were very rich looking. He usually looked better than Pa. This being the case, it was a shock to us to find a discrepancy in his dress, in church, of all places—the toughest place of all to hold back a laugh, or a rumbling stomach.

The minister was expounding in great detail on Noah, while we were wondering if the "Let us pray" would ever come. Suddenly Teedy motioned for us to look at Billy's feet. It was then we discovered the famous dresser had on odd socks. This was like Zsa Zsa Gabor with only one false eyelash.

Looking at each other and at half a dozen friends surrounding us, we started snickering. Meeting another's eye for even two seconds would start us laughing. Billy was getting madder and madder because he couldn't figure out what we were laughing about. We tried everything we could think of to smother that laugh, but the more we tried to suppress it, the louder we snorted it out. Our guffaws ceased in a hurry when the minister stopped in the middle of the sermon and said, "Could you people tell me what the joke is?"

"We just noticed Billy has on odd socks," I blurted out. The minister's face is graced with a smile, verging on a laugh as he says, "Well can you please keep it down." By this time Billy is looking down in astonishment at his feet. "My God," whispers Billy as he sinks way down in the pew, knowing the eyes of the dentist's and doctor's daughters are on him. "Why didn't you tell me about my socks?" He's almost lying on the seat now. Getting our laughter under control, we watch the minister disinterestedly for a few minutes—then look down to see Billy on his hands and knees on the floor. "What is he going to do now, take someone's sock?" He inches his way out to the aisle, with a threatening wave of his fist—meaning for us not to look at him, or he'll choke us. We know enough to comply with Billy's orders, as he had the quickest temper of the lot, and if riled might tear our pew out by its roots, with us in it.

Out of the corner of our eye, we can see him slithering down the aisle to the door, almost on his belly. We are on the far side of the church, so the people on the opposite side think it's a ghost, or an act of God, as the door of the church opens and closes, apparently by itself.

When church was over, we rushed out, thinking Billy was so ashamed, he'd left early to commit suicide. Instead we found him at home eating. When we asked him why he left the way he did, he said, "Did you think I was going to stay til the end and mingle with all those girls looking at my socks?" "Well you might as well have, what do you think was the most embarrassing—wearing odd socks, or crawling out of the church on your belly?" Billy pulled up his pantlegs to show off a sporty pair of matching socks. We had our answer, and I now know that Billy, if he had found out he was improperly garbed, would have crept out of Buckingham Palace on his belly.

Before each service everything seemed funny to us. There were some real characters coming in along with older people stubbing their toes or dropping their hats, and we saw it all. When with Pa, we trained ourselves to laugh hysterically without a sound coming out, and an almost completely sober face, except for a little twitching around the corner of the mouth, now and then. It only took one twitch for Pa's eyes to tell us to keep quiet. I often wondered how Pa could keep such a straight face and not join in with us. Not much chance of that though, unless Pa suddenly went foolish.

Sometimes there would be a small noise from the rear, not much, but enough of a stir that we couldn't keep our heads at attention. We were dying to look behind us, which nearly caused our spines to snap.

The fourth brother from Pa was Billy, who seemed able to twist his head without moving his neck. This enabled him to peek at any commotion that occurred; and relay the message back to us with his eyes, in Morse code fashion.

Getting more comfortable, Pa would uncross his legs and clear his throat, to be followed by four hacking frogs, trying to fall in line with Pa's, so he'd think it was only himself. With the exception of Murray—second from Pa. Murray would give it another hack. As the first had only awakened the frog, the second hack would clear it. And none too soon, because if Murray had tried another hack, Pa would have beheaded Murray's frog once and for all.

Then the choir in their flowing robes and graduation hats would float down the aisle, looking straight ahead. The choir is seated, and Pa looks at us as if to say, "Try to stay awake." The minister, standing, raises his hands above his head and we hope he is going to shoot right up through the roof of the church, like Superman, or make a jackknife dive into the congregation. But instead, he murmurs, "Let us pray." With no interest whatsoever in what the minister is saying, this is our moment of relief as his head is bowed and we are at ease, kicking each others' feet. Our pious Pa at this moment has his head almost between his knees, studying the bottom of the pew, which gives us a good chance to look around—even to go as far as looking directly behind us, at the kid with the runny nose and his homely sister Irma. We often wished that this opening prayer lasted at least half an hour, instead of only minutes, so we wouldn't be afflicted with muscle cramps from having to sit as though paralyzed when Pa was on guard.

At first, after hearing the benediction, we used to say "Thanks", until Pa told us how ashamed he was when one of us muttered it rather loudly. But we were very thankful to get out on those Sunday mornings, and if we had been wealthy, we'd have offered the minister a bribe to close the church forever. Then it was Sunday school in the afternoons, and again to church with Pa in the evenings, so you see why we loved the Sabbath so. We spent more time in church than the minister and the pews.

Mussolini's Cap

We just couldn't win where Sundays were concerned, and we were even forbidden to throw snowballs on this day. One Sunday evening during a mild spell the snow was excellent for snowballs. On the way from church, Pa was held up by an associate, talking mine. We walked on by ourselves, dressed to the teeth, and took the longer route home. Pa never took the long way home, so we knew we'd be safe.

Mixing with a few boys who were throwing snowballs, we joined in. Our targets were whoever passed by. In the distance came a figure wearing what looked like the dress cap Mussolini wore before he was dragged through the streets of Italy. Confident that Pa had taken his usual route, I screeched a command, "Here comes Mussolini, let him have it," as the hail of snowballs splattered our beloved Pa. There was nothing to do but hide. Pa continued toward home, with us thinking he'd never guess it was us. Billy was home as it was his turn to tend Pearl, and Pa sent him to look for us. When we entered the house we could smell what was in store. Looking in the window first was enough. We could see the shade of red on Pa's face. May God have mercy on our rears. I was first this time, which was good, as the human arm, knowing it has two to go, can only swing violently for a little while. As he was belting it to me on the rear, he kept saying, "We'll see who Mussolini is." After he finished with the rest, we slithered to bed and lay on our stomachs wondering why it couldn't have been Pa they dragged through the streets of Italy.

With the experience we had in stripping, getting whippings, and going to bed early, we should have been either burlesque queens, tennis balls, or stand-ins for Rip Van Winkle.

Baked Stuffed Shoes

One pair of Sunday boots a year was added to our wardrobe, and it was usually a Saturday night when Pa bought these boots at the Co-operative. We four brothers knew we were due for a pair of Crosby's high black boots at two-ninety-eight a pair whenever Pa asked us the size of our old Sunday boots. Teedy and Billy remembered their correct size and spoke up quickly before Pa changed his mind on the subject. Murray and I seemed to have a mental block, but managed to mumble some kind of size to Pa. It wasn't until Pa left for the store that we looked at our worn size twelves. By then it was too late to tell Pa that he had us down for size elevens.

We were tickled to have the new shiny boots when Pa came back and fitted us into them. Even though we had to curl our toes and grit our teeth we didn't let Pa know, and when he'd look us in the eye, we'd say, "They fit good." Pa would have had to return them on Monday, wearless, if we had told him they pinched, and then not only would we not have had new boots for Sunday, but we'd have had a disgruntled Pa, who would have forced us to take up residence in another part of the globe where no footwear was needed.

What a time we had next day going to church with Pa. Billy and Teedy strode beside Pa, like normal walkers, while my twin and I followed behind lame and unbalanced, as though we were in ladies' high heel shoes. If Pa happened to look around, we'd do the impossible and walk straight. The agony we had to endure for a whole year wasn't something we looked forward to. I suggested to Murray that we'd be more comfortable wearing them sideways.

When we got home we made straight for Ma and told her the whole story. Ma suggested we trade boots. (Why didn't we think of this up behind the church?) The switch was made for better or worse. Murray had the changed boots on much faster than I, and with a contented look, he strut around the room like a Bantie Rooster. "Don't hurt a bit," says Murray, smiling for the first time since he touched the boots. A happy look settled over Ma's features, as she knew they could never be exchanged after walking a mile to church, not to mention Pa. Murray couldn't keep still and kept running around the small room to show the change while I was knotting my second boot string. When I stood up, I was like a person who had never had ice skates on before, trying to balance on my new footwear. I plummeted back down on my seat. Ma took hold of my arm, helped me to my feet, as though handling a baby just learning to walk, and led me for a few steps. I walked like I had half a bowling ball strapped to each foot. Ma left the room. There was nothing more she could do, so she went back to setting the table while I was wondering whether Pa would notice if I cut the front out and painted my toes the same colour as the boots.

With both feet doubled up, I zoomed into the kitchen behind Pa's back and planked myself on a chair at the table, praying he wouldn't ask me to get him a glass of water or, God forbid, do a tap dance. Next to me, Murray, with a half titter, was giving me light taps on my swollen feet with his loose shoes.

But with Ma's help that Sunday, things didn't go too bad. After dinner, she told me to go up to my room and stay there until the kids came back from Sunday school. She said she'd take Pa over to the neighbours and keep him there for awhile.

Running through the house without shoes on before my brothers arrived home from church, I had never felt so free. At times I could have run up the wall and across the ceiling like a fly. But it wasn't long before I heard mixed voices in the yard. The door opened and there confronting me were six new boots, which I hated the sight of by now. Fleet of foot, I followed them upstairs. After they removed their suits and had carefully hung them up, they placed their boots below. They weren't to be worn again until next Sunday, so I could foresee a happy week for me as it was Pa's law we wear our old boots to school, and my old ones, though tongueless, (it would have been better if Pa had been tongueless) were very comfortable.

So I planned immediately for next Sunday, as I knew Ma would run out of ways to protect me. A conversation with an old Armenian woman gave me a procedure for stretching boots, and thank heavens it wasn't patting them with cow manure. She told me to soak the boots in water all night, then next morning while they were still wet to stuff the toes of the boots with slices of raw potatoes, and let them dry there.

Like a night nurse on duty, I worked on the solution. Cutting up two large potatoes, I placed them in a little bag until morning. Next morning with daylight seeping into the room, I sought out my experiment. When I saw those small boots dunked in the water bucket, they didn't look much bigger than the potatoes I was to stuff in the toe. How would they ever dry in time? But Ma came to the rescue. After I had placed the potatoes in the toes, she took the boots downstairs and laid them on the oven door of the coal stove. There they sat all day.

Late that afternoon, before Pa came home from work, Teedy was busy getting kindling in for the morning fire. The kindling was damp so he pushed it into the oven to dry out while the stove was still hot. Had he taken an eye-level armful of kindling, Teedy might have seen my boots, but with a double armful over his eyes, he just guessed at the opening of the

52

oven, and shoved it all in, right along with my wet, stuffed boots. The oven door was closed, mostly to prevent Pa from hitting his shins, and another shovelful of coal was thrown on.

Before retiring each night, Pa's last words always were, "Is the kindling out of the oven?" as one time we forgot about it and had to throw a bucket of water in the oven. "I'll take them out," I said. Then it dawned on me, "Good Lord, where are my boots?"

Almost shoving Pa down the stairs as he was coming up to bed, I flew to the kitchen and pulled down the oven door. What looked like two shrivelled bats met my eyes. Crinkled, turned up, and shrunk, my boots sported a flaky baked potato in each toe. A new dish was born—baked stuffed boots. We were all scared. Secret discussions were called, with Ma as consultant. I could barely get the potatoes out of the boot, let alone get my foot in. I couldn't have worn those turned-up-toed boots unless I cut off my foot and sharpened my ankle. Pa would have thought I was turning into an elf. So we started with the price of the boots. Small donations were accepted, Ma giving the Ivory soap percentage. To town I raced the next day in my well-worn old boots. I didn't have to be warned about the size to get, as I almost plunked my two feet in the clerk's mouth, and said, "Two sizes larger than my foot, please." Happily, like a spirited horse (even whinnying a few times) I trotted home from town hours before Pa arrived from the coal mine. I placed my new larger-sized boots in their proper position beside the others.

In a challenging mood, I dared Sunday to come now, knowing the room I had in those new Crosbys. Even my brothers had a contented look as I slipped each eager foot into the new boots.

On our way home from Sunday school this day,

53

Murray drew my attention to a gathering of people. It was a funeral procession for a not-too-well-off miner. "Let's go see," said Murray. Murray was a lover of funerals. I followed him like a puppy dog.

A funeral procession was different in those days. The deceased was usually kept at home for three days until the day of the funeral at which time the hearse—a chariot affair with curtains on the wide glass windows and the coffin exposed to the onlookers lining the road—was pulled by a team of two fiery black horses. The men would march in twos like in a parade, as many as fifty or more, then a car or two, then another parade of men. The better-known the deceased, the larger the number of walkers.

However, after the undertaker had lined up the few men and boys that were gathered, this procession looked quite small. It was two miles to the graveyard from this home, and Murray, not wanting to miss any tears, thought we should make the small procession look bigger, and enter ourselves. It only took one whisper from Murray with his hand cupped over his mouth saying "Let's march" for me to agree. With my comfortable boots on, I could have walked to Ethiopia. The sidewalks were lined with friends of the dead person taking their last look. Our small chests bulged with pride to be in the procession.

Only about three blocks on our way, walking at a parrot's pace, I could see Murray was trying to tell me something. No one talked while marching, just kept a straight ahead sombre look in their eyes, with the expression "Why did it happen to him?" Murray's eyes were still trying to tell me something, and it wasn't "Why did it happen to him?" It was "Why did it happen to me?" He just wasn't wearing that happy look that he usually displayed at other funerals. The look was urgent. Finally I noticed he kept trying to kick one leg up while marching. "Don't tell me his boots are hurting him!" I thought, or was this a new dance step he was trying out. But I knew the symptoms.

Once you got in the lineup it was a catastrophe to drop out. You'd feel like an Indian giver. But things were worsening for Murray. So I got a message to him, "They'll slow down at the railroad crossing, then you can take your boots off." Murray's face filled out, hiding the pain wrinkles.

Stopping for the railroad track, I never saw anyone scuff two boots from two feet so fast, and he let out a deep shaky breath that he must have been holding back for the past ten minutes. With nearly a mile to go in his sock feet, Murray tucked the too tight little boots under his left arm, which left the right arm free to swing, making it appear to onlookers that he may have been carrying a wreath in the left. It was a good thing it wasn't winter, or Murray would have had to continue the walk with his boots on. Then I would have had to carry him home to be placed in a wheel chair for the rest of his life.

After the funeral, Murray carried his boots to within fifty feet of our house, and then put them back on. With me in the lead, I took him the right track out of Pa's sight. Under no circumstances was I going to trade mine with him again, as with the space I now had in mine, I could have gotten Pa's foot in there and still have had room for a sofa and chair. Murray continued to put damp potatoes in his, which never did much good; and for a year of Sundays, he hobbled around out of Pa's reach. Ma just couldn't find enough to pay his tab. But once a week was all he suffered; and everything was cosy for Pa, as he'd smile at the eight little boots, nestling under the suits, never noticing that one tiny pair smelt of wet spuds, or that Murray who was the wiriest of all of us when barefooted, would almost turn to stone each time he locked his feet into his Crosbys.

The Little Metal Man

For each of our three Sunday donations, a big penny was given to us. I now realize it must have been mostly to make a noise on the collection plate to prove you had given your contribution. "But who said I was going to give up that prize?" We hated to part with our big pennies, and usually didn't. The only store open on Sunday was old Mr. Allen's, and he was a good mile from the church. That's where they should have held Sunday school if they were after my prize, because that's where my penny always ended up.

We would usually meet after Sunday school to buy a penny jawbreaker, red or orange, and almost as large as a golf ball—much too large for an ordinary mouth. Luckily we were blessed with large mouths, so we'd slip it in, and it would last for hours. After a couple of hours sucking, something told you to roll it over in your mouth. This was quite a trick, because it would get caught in the inside of your jaw and cause terrific pain. One day it took our six hands plus Teedy's two to pry one out of Teedy's mouth. He thought we had removed his tonsils.

When going into Mr. Allen's store to buy my jawbreaker, I always had a guilty conscience, scared he might say some Sunday, "Well, is this your collection for Sunday school?" If he had he would have made a profit, as the big penny would have been left spinning on the floor as I spun out the door.

When collection had to be parted with, the Sunday

school teacher would line us up single file and we'd walk around her desk to where there was a miniature rocking chair with a little metal man in it, his arms innocently folded. In the crook of one of his greedy little arms was a slit, and when money was placed in the opening he would nod his head in thanks, chuckling under his breath. We knew after studying this mechanical phenomenon that we could master it. And that little man wasn't going to get our penny, even if he reached out and grabbed us with his little metal arm.

So we found out how to get the nod of thanks, and still keep our penny for Mr. Allen's jawbreakers. We would get a rich kid in front of us, one who was slow and easy going; and when he'd place his nickel or dime in, we'd brush him out of the way, touch the metal arm, and naturally we would get the nod, and a sarcastic look.

We only spent a year in that room, and it was a good thing, because if I remember correctly not only did we cheat on our offering, but at one time had planned to kidnap the little man lock, stock and rocking chair—and crack open the take between us.

Deafen The Minister, Murray

Meanwhile when the rest of the kids in the neighbourhood were out snowballing or playing some games on Sunday, we'd be making our third trip to church in one day to the "sleepy service" as Teedy called the night visit. Sitting close to the front, the minister could tell that each of our back teeth was decayed (too bad he wasn't a dentist), because as soon as he had finished his opening prayer, four tired kids, looking directly at him and the choir, yawned constantly, hoping to make them tired too so they'd send everybody home to bed. Glancing sideways without moving our heads, we'd see a couple of kids alone, no fathers with them. Their heads would be spinning in all directions, each whispering to the other, probably about us being stuck there with Pa. So we'd sit up straight, and pretend we were happy and proud to be there with Pa, all the while wishing Pa would come down with an attack of influenza and disintegrate.

During these church services with Pa, those big cents meant for the collection plate were a great temptation to keep. If the man who took the collection started from Billy's end working over to Pa, then four big cents adorned the plate. But if he started from Pa's end and worked our way, the last one in line kept his big penny and his life as long as Pa didn't catch him.

The one time we were quite willing to give up our collection, I managed to lose mine. Many times in Sunday school and church, there would be much praise for Murray and I for really belting out the hymns in tune. (They say this talent is acquired through frequent jawbreaker sucking.) One year for a special Easter service we graduated from the congregation to the choir because of this outburst.

Being in the choir had a few advantages. We could see everyone in the church without having to turn our heads around sneakily, and all we had to see of the preacher was his back and the seat of his pants. Then we could sit back, relax and fantasize about an invisible foot kicking him in the seat of the pants, out of the pulpit, into the congregation, and onto Pa's lap.

The one drawback was that we needed a special silver offering, instead of our large penny. Though wages were taking small jumps over the years, not so the collection from Pa. Neither Murray nor I could summon up courage to ask Pa. (Now today I'd take a good shot of scotch and face Pa, except he's dead.) We even thought of painting the penny, but Pa had used the last of the silver paint to make the rusty stove pipe look new.

Instead on the eventful day, I suggested to Murray we search the water-swept roads to see what we could find, as this time of year, with snow melting and ruts in the roads becoming gushing canals, was a good time to find anything from coins to watches to little kids lost in the winter snows.

Soon I had found a small Victorian five-cent piece, a masterpiece today. Feeling rich with my new found coin, I ran toward the church. Perfectly groomed with my shoes shining like rosy apples, a sudden three-foot ditch in front of me wasn't going to slow down my progress, much. I leaped across and landed on the other side, less about six inches; and while grappling to save my pants and shirt from becoming too drenched, I lost not only the five-cent piece, but also my big penny. We searched and searched in two feet of very cold water. I thought I could see better if I put my head under, but it was hopeless as one ear was turning white. At least Murray still had his big cent— its indentation was unmistakably outside his envelope. Murray added his name, omitting the amount. I drooled my empty envelope shut and into the church I dripped, thinking that after church I'd go back, rope off the eight feet of ditch and continue my search for the five-cent piece and the penny.

Down the aisle and up into the choir we marched. Hymns came out of us as loud as wildcat screeches, hoping to deafen the minister so he'd forget to take up the collection. It had to come sometime, and after reading the different meetings of the week, the preacher said in a low voice, "The offering will now be taken." Murray turned and looked me straight in the eye. Not waiting to see who would take up the collection in the choir, Murray leaped to his feet, grabbed the plate, and passed it to each individual as if he were a full-fledged deacon. My heart stopped pounding as he came to pick up my well-sealed lifeless envelope, as I knew we would be home and well hid before the counting began.

We decided to lower our singing voices after this service, so that by the time next Easter rolled around we wouldn't be picked for the choir, because the next time they might decide to open each offering as soon as it was dropped on the plate to see if everyone had given the amount shown. Then I'd have had to stand up and point an accusing finger at Pa, saying, "That man wouldn't give us any silver offering." After which I'd have had to hide out in the church for the rest of my days. Pa wouldn't have dared kill me in the church.

Our Card Of Star
Going to church three times each Sunday from early Fall until the end of school was not enough for us. Some white-collared churchgoers, thinking the young ones never got enough Bible learning, decided to start a summer Bible school. Getting rid of day school was a joyous occasion, but to be sucked right back into a Bible school, especially in summer, was like being rescued from a burning building only to be whisked away to the electric chair. Pa received notice of the Bible school and certainly didn't answer negatively. Of course, you couldn't blame Pa. He was just trying to make saints out of his little gangsters.

This was a Presbyterian set-up, and I would have gladly become a Hindu to avoid that summer prison deal. The rest of our friends of different faiths were as free as the seagulls, running up and down cliffs scuffing their best shoes, with us wishing they had Pa for a father and we had theirs. We would have traded Pa for any drunkard to change our scene.

We were to assemble in the large church five days a week all summer, from nine until twelve. The older members of the church were proud to be parents of these fine young people. We thought of it as a trap to stunt our deviltry. But no matter how they set their trap, we thought of ways to spring it.

I didn't mind attending the first gathering. I was always good at gathering. But after the first two days Teedy and I found this Bible study took a great bite out of our personal affairs during the much-too-short summer months when we should have been free from loudmouthed teachers and homework. And instead of bare feet, overalls, and sleeveless shirts, which we felt at ease in skipping around the shores on the warm summer mornings, each morning found us sporting our Sunday best. We felt really out of place, dressing up on these foreign days. But Pa was all for it and gave us the go-ahead to wear our Sunday suits, so there was no alternative though we felt far from religious.

Roughly five hundred children met the first day, and it took the whole day to register for the coming weeks. Pa stayed home from work to make sure we were amongst the many attending this unwanted function. So this day we were dressing not only for the ministers and deacons we'd meet, but also for Pa, who watched for even a crossed brace on our pants.

The first day Teedy and I found hard to endure, even though it was only our names they were interested in. Murray and Billy, for some reason, seemed to enjoy the atmosphere, maybe because there were plenty of girls there. The second day was too much for Teedy and I after we found out what we had to do, and where we were to go. First, they put us in a class full of the homeliest girls in North America. They had to have been hand picked. I'm sure the minister came to the teacher and said, "OK, now we'll put all the really hideous people in this class so as not to mar the other classes." The classes next to us had devoured all the pretty girls while we were being smothered by Cinderella's stepsisters. They soon shoved two other males in with us who needed no classification as they were even homelier than us.

Next, each kid was given ten or twelve small books of the Bible and he was to learn a page a night of each book, which naturally filled our hearts with delight. You were to receive stars at the end of each week, according to how many questions you answered right. But who wanted to read about Job's suffering in the boiling heat of the summer? If they had thrown in a few jokes here and there, I would have been all for it. But what with all the Zebediah, Ezekiel, and Zachariah stuff, a computer would have had trouble just trying to spell them. Teedy and I made sure we received the little books, not because we wanted to study them, but because they were free.

I wouldn't even study when I was at home on a cold winter's night yet here they were pushing those little books at us to study that night, when all I had on my mind were beautiful summer night love breezes.

Small golden stars were to be added to a certificate you were presented with the first day; and somehow someone gave Teedy and I each a star—must have been for remembering our right name.

But like I said, the second day was our limit, new clothes or not. Each morning we'd walk with Billy and

62

Murray, erect and mannerly while Pa watched, but a fair distance from our house we'd make a complete U-turn for the shores despite the coaxing of Billy and Murray to go on with them.

Now down at the shores our friends thought Teedy and I were turning into queers because there we would appear bright and early each morning dressed like mafia kingpins. We only took their insults for a day or two. Then we began taking our old clothes and changing rapidly in a cave, like Superman in his phone booth, after which we'd join our buddies in their messy attire.

Around noon, upon seeing an army of dapper dudes, led by Billy and Murray, marching from the church, Teedy and I would scoot for the cave, dress hurriedly and fall into line with them toward home.

After the first week, we received quite a shock when Billy and Murray showed us how many stars they had in comparison to our lone one. If we had only known then that in any bookstore you could buy a hundred stars for ten cents.

What a sickening feeling it was when Billy and Murray told us that at the end of four weeks all the parents and children were to gather in the church and the kids were to bring their card of stars for the minister to announce. Teedy and I, with our *card of star*, thought we should go the remaining few days so we would fit in a little better with the rest.

But each morning the big red sun peeked out of the east and seemed to say, "It's going to be a hot one today." And as if the two of us had heard the sun speak we'd hit for the shores again, change from the dashing groom to the unworried tramp, and soak up the sun and salt air until noon.

At night we were so scared thinking of what Pa

would do to us on that dreadful morning that we'd dream about those windy-named characters in the Bible and mumble to each other about them all night.

The final day, when we were to face Pa in church, had to come. No trip to the shore this Sunday morning. Murray's and Billy's cards were glittering with stars, while our star was becoming dull to look at. We had even failed to make duplicates out of it by pressing wax paper on it and drawing around it. But there was Pa, shaving and attaching his collar to his shirt with studs, and us scurrying around the house dressed like little bishops.

Eleven a.m. was zero hour when we'd be cowering around darling Pa waiting for the minister to call off the names and number of stars, after which we knew Pa would make sure that we experienced Job's suffering personally and would see to it that we saw all the stars we wanted.

It is now ten-thirty and twitching and nervous we shine our shoes for the last walk to the gallows. Twenty minutes before the eleventh hour, the telephone rings; Billy answers it and says in a mannerly voice (mostly because he's dressed up), "It's for you Pa." Straightening his necktie, Pa walks the short hallway to the phone. Eight ears are straining to hear the conversation. A smile of relief washes over our faces, as we hear Pa say to the man on the other end, "Well you come and pick me up." This was our reprieve. Pa was going to Sydney, fifteen miles away to a union meeting; and while we knew and cared little about unions, we would have gladly joined one then. And if they hadn't agreed to come and pick Pa up, we would have volunteered to push Pa there in the wheelbarrow, non stop.

Teedy and I went willingly to church with Billy and

Murray, albeit in haphazard fashion, clutching our one-starred card under our arm. I was so happy I wouldn't have refused if the minister had told me I'd have to sing every verse of "The Old Rugged Cross" in Lebanese; as long as Teedy could accompany me on the comb, as that's all he could play.

The minister called the names alphabetically, but when the M's were finished, Teedy and I still hadn't moved from our seats. We stuck it out though, figuring he may have put us with the Z's, under Zachariah. When there was no mention of us there, we still hugged our seats. We knew our names weren't going to be called after the benediction, as the crowd was dispersing, so with a dignified air and a tight grip on our card, we arose and followed Murray and Billy out of the church, thinking, "Well done my good and faithful servant."

When Pa returned from the meeting he asked us all about the special service, and wanted to see our cards. Murray and Billy proudly handed their cards to Pa, while Teedy and I just as proudly told Pa that we had more stars (we were counting the stars in the sky) than any of the other kids—(which we would have had, if we'd had the money to buy the box of stars) so the minister had decided to keep ours, as a souvenir of the Bible school. . . .

Get Him Quick While He's Out Of His Mind
The only fun thing about Sunday school was the picnics held yearly. We were taken by boat for five miles to a spot that was like another planet to us. Peanut butter sandwiches were packed by our sisters. I'm not an avid lover of peanut butter today, but whenever I smell it my mind wanders back forty-five years to those picnics.

The boat rides were usually rough, and I wasn't too brave. So I'd keep close to a heavyset man or woman in case trouble arose. They might drown but they wouldn't sink, and I could hold onto their blimp-like figures until help came. But we always managed to get there without calamity, and I'd walk dreamily up to the field where we were to picnic.

The night before, Diamond Jim Pa would give each of us a quarter for our treats at the picnic. The quarter never got cold, because from the minute we got it in our hand we'd sleep with it all night reciting the things we would buy the next day. First we would buy an iron brew—the taste I still remember. Even half a teaspoonful curled around your taste buds and sent thoughts of wonderment through your mind. Then would come the ice cream. (I can still feel the cold cream dripping down my chin, as the sweet maple flavour slid down my throat.) Then in greedy glee I'd think, "Oh Lord, what next?"—a nut bar, and I still have ten cents left.

At the picnic next day I'm pondering how to spend my last dime when I see Murray running towards me. He tells me about this stupid guy they've put in charge of the ice cream booth. Murray says he gave him a quarter for an ice cream, and the guy gave him back forty-five cents change. Murray drags me along by the arm, whispering, "Get him quick while he's out of his mind!" Up I run with my dime; he hands me my ice cream and twenty cents change. A new world has opened up for me. (We should have gotten this guy a job at the store close to our house.) I ate the ice cream so fast, I hardly had time to enjoy it. Up I ran again, and got another twenty-five cents in change. It was like a lucky day in Las Vegas! I made a profit of sixty-five cents, Murray hitting the eighty cent mark, and we ate like Henry the Eighth, especially Murray, since he was the reincarnation of Henry.

At seven p.m. the boat would give a couple of toots at the wharf. The mournful sound could be heard miles away and wherever you were you'd make a bee-line to the boat, and float home tired and full but with a good day under your belt. The trip home was a sad one, knowing it would be a full year before the picnic took place again.

At first we thought we'd never eat again we were so stuffed. But after a few hours on the boat, reaching home at nine, with our digestive motor ticking over once again, we'd get ourselves something we thought we'd never touch again—a slice of homemade bread, drenched in molasses.

Chapter Three

You Win A Few,
You Lose Most Of Them

The Hen That Was A Crow

Teedy and I always wanted a hen, and with all the kids in our family we wished that just one time Ma could have given birth to a hen. Just to see one that belonged to someone else would almost stop our breathing. If we could only have one we'd never want anything else in the world, except food.

We'd even ask hen owners if they'd sell us one or two, but I guess they knew we never had the price of an egg, and would never give us an answer.

Then Teedy told me about this old deserted grave-yard that was loaded with live chickens. There was a look in his eye as if to say, "And no one owns them." But he knew the old man in the red house close by owned them, and I knew it too.

Early one June morning, he and I started out to hen-nap one of these hens. Chasing them about a mile in different directions we soon found out that small chickens have much more maneuverability and speed than a grown hen. Falling over the aged tombstones never lessened our pursuit. Finally the chickens gravitated toward their home quarters, and we ended up herding them right into their own barn. Arousing the old man, he opened a squeaky door and gave the command, "Get um", while what looked like a small buffalo galloped toward us, growling savagely. This German police dog rushed at us while we flew toward a vacant unlocked car nearby. With the dog snapping at our heels we fell into the car breathless and henless.

Quite at home now, as the dog had retreated, we saw our old family doctor coming toward us. We sputtered out our adventure, and explained why we were sitting in his car. Easygoing and a family man, he soon understood our predicament. Patting us lovingly on the head, he smiled and said, "I'm glad the car wasn't locked, and that man should post a 'Beware of buffalo' sign."

Still obsessed with the desire to own a hen or two, Teedy and I watched every move of anyone who owned hens, and studied the upkeep of their flocks. Then one day Teedy came to me all excited. He had found out about a certain man who owned fifty or more hens hemmed in a small wire coop, about ten-foot square and six-foot high, and that they were starving with no water and the temperature was in the eighties. With the thoughts, "Those hens are suffering, and what good care we can give them," we were out to get one.

Teedy said they were so hungry that if you put your hand over the fence they'd fly up and grab on to it. Our plan was to go over just before roosting time and I'd surrender my fingers over the top of the high coop (a very unnerving experience) and see what I could latch on to. Looking around in four directions to see if the coast was clear, I spied a block of wood that was used by the old man to decapitate the hens, a few black feathers clinging to the dried blood. The fence was much higher than me, so I grabbed the block and pushed it close to the fence. Reaching over, I was grabbed by the sleeve and fingers by three hungry hens. I felt like screaming that I had been attacked by a buzzard. I managed to hold on to one and shook the other two off. As I flung my prey over to my side of the fence, the block tumbled and I fell flat on my stomach, still holding onto our prize, though I squashed it a bit. But the hen's eyelids were moving which was a sign that there was still life there.

Darkness was setting in. As I carried the hen toward Teedy, the lookout man, about fifty feet from me, he began signalling frantically. A kid is sauntering toward him. Teedy is trying desperately to tell me to get lost until he gets rid of the kid. I soon catch on and slither under an old door leaning against the shed, the hen stuffed deep down in my bosom. Teedy walks toward the kid much faster than he is coming toward Teedy. I'm well hid but deathly squawks are coming from the hen, who would much rather have been stolen by a fox, or any other kind of animal who didn't try to kill it's prey by squashing it to death. Teedy is talking a loud, blue streak to the kid and edging him down the road away from my hideout. I'm all cramped up, sweating, and starting to itch. Lice from his louse-laden hen are finding their way to my mouth.

Teedy and the kid's voices are getting fainter. I crawl out from under the door, trying not to put too much pressure on the nearly-suffocated, pancaked hen. Getting to my feet, I swish the lice from my mouth. Reaching under my shirt, I can feel my chest all scratched to pieces. I soon brought forth what looked like a dieting crow—two pounds of feathers, beak and all, and a large pair of yellowed feet.

Darkness is upon us, and I feel at ease, but not chest-wise. A faint whistle comes from Teedy, a signal that the coast is clear. A small silhoutte in front of the street light turns out to be Teedy's stubby frame coming toward me. "It's OK he's gone," were wonderful words to hear in my predicament. "Have you got her?" "Right here, and I believe she's dead." But her eyes were still moving.

Beating it toward home, he and I walked guiltily, suspicious of every sound. Since this was Saturday night, we knew Pa would be out for the evening and we'd have the house to ourselves. I placed the hen gently on the floor. The twenty-five watt bulb was too much for its eyes. It stood awhile, then dropped to the floor. Teedy quickly administered first aid. I held its useless beak open, while he poured the melted butter-cure down its larynx while it swallowed to prevent itself from gagging. Minutes after this administration the hen gave a few clucks and we knew it would survive as it straightened up and sort of yawned, as if to say, "You know I could stand a cold drink of something."

My shirt was crawling with lice, and I stripped to my shorts. Teedy and I had very guilty consciences now, and worried that the owner might notice his loss. Finally I decided that what we should do was to cut its large tail off so the owner wouldn't recognize it as one of his. A few hacks here and there and it would never look like its other starving sisters, who also had no weight, and empty craws, but with enormous tails.

Teedy held the squawking bird, while I detailed it with the scissors. It was surprising how this changed the look of the Louse Giver. But we still couldn't shake the feeling of dread: that the man might miss it tonight. Fear won over our love for the hen and we decided to take it back the same night. I put on a different shirt and Miss Hen got a new carrying case, an onion bag. We rapped at the man's door at ten p.m., and asked if he'd lost one of his hens. Speaking without concern and bored by the intrusion he said, "Put it on the floor." Then he added, "Oh no, all mine have long tails, but throw it in with the rest anyway." So our crow was put back with its sisters. All the way we grieved about our mistake, as the man wasn't even thankful we had brought back our prize possession; and all I had for a reward was a handful of black tail feathers, and lice bites all over my chest. In a few days when everything blew over, we sauntered over to throw a little feed into the hen we had embarrassed a little, to find the owner inside the coop, with an object in his hand, slashing right and left. Acting unconcerned we walked toward him, and found out a new way to capture a hen. He had a three-foot dip net in his hand, and with one swipe a hen would land in the net. We were flabbergasted at how easy it was to catch a hen and our minds began wandering to where we could posssibly pick up a dip net in case the urge never left us.

The Pip

All our young lives our interest in hens continued, and it's a good thing it didn't run over into our adult lives, or we'd all have married hens. We lived on a building lot that had just barely enough extra room for a patch-quilt henhouse which we constructed from scraps we found on the shores, before we even had a hen to put in it.

In order to buy a hen we had to have fifty cents, which was hard to come by in those days. But blueberry picking time was at hand. Picking berries from morning until night our hearts were on the hen we would buy, and we made enough to get one hen.

The inside of the henhouse we built was a palace. We even had a mirror for the hen, and we would watch the hen gazing into it. Sometimes the hen would stare for a minute or more. That kept it from being lonesome, as in the mirror it had another hen with it, although only a ghost.

We'd go out to the henpen and sit for hours. We could almost read the hen's mind. To find one egg in the nest lined with cloth, next to the door knob, was one of the nicest things we could ask for. Then to find one under the roost was even lovelier to the heart. Teedy and I studied the hen so long we soon learned the moment the egg was to be dropped. The hen would sit up in the nest, like a penguin, then in seconds the egg would drop.

One summer in particular, I was the only one who had a hen and I was happy. I would sit beside her and try to lay right along with her. I'd watch her while she strutted around admiring herself in the mirror, and when she'd lie down in the coal dust and ruffle her feathers, I'd ruffle mine right along with her. Then early one morning, I walked out to find my sweet speckled hen had died during the night. I barely recall when the King of England died, though it was years after my hen tragedy, but my dear hen's death remains vivid in my memory. Her disease was diagnosed as "The Pip" by Teedy, who was then about nine. There weren't many vets in those days, but I'm sure the few that were around told all their secrets to my younger brother.

He told me this was an almost sure death disease, as he had heard the adults talking. He said a lump came on the hen's tongue, and you had to open its beak and slide the lump off with a rolled silk handkerchief. That was the only cure. I figured it would have died anyway, as we never had a cotton handkerchief, let alone a silk one. We interred the hen with a terrific ceremony, though we were somewhat disgusted, as we only had chicken once a year, and there was all that meat going under the ground to fertilize the small garden we had which yielded yearly about three strawberries and five potatoes.

A few hymns were sung, Billy threw the ashes to ashes on the grave. (Ashes weren't rationed. We burnt coal, so everywhere you looked were ashes.) Then a meeting was held by us four to try to get me a new hen. They all had great intentions at the time of the funeral, with promises to buy me a whole hennery, but they soon forgot after a day or two. I continued to endure that summer with a cracked heart, not quite broken. Every time I thought of that terrible disease, it was worse to me than the 1917 flu epidemic, and I vowed that when I grew up I would go into the silk handkerchief business, in case Teedy ever caught the pip.

The Day We Lost Our Holes

Hens were out of our thoughts now. We were getting a new mattress. New mattresses were the main topic about once every fifteen years. So when we overheard a conversation between Ma and Pa, that they should get a new mattress as the boys' bed was getting rather worn, we knew we were the boys, so we did a few cartwheels. I almost had to gag Murray in school so he wouldn't raise his hand and tell the teacher, and the fifty pupils, we were to get one.

A health inspector wouldn't have had trouble condemning the one we four had slept on for a decade. It had eight pockets. These were tunneled out by four sharp feet at the top and four at the bottom, as we slept two up, two down. After settling down into our bed, our feet found our holes and a not-too-warm foot would enter, first one then the other one, just like settling your feet into saddle stirrups, and it would be only minutes until snugness took over. "Are you in your holes?" was usually the last grammar recited before the snoring began. "Just wait now," was the reply from Teedy. Then, "OK"—everyone was happy. We said goodnight—everyone had their holes and we were ready for take-off.

One evening the cooperative horse and wagon reined into the yard, and along with our gallon of molasses, and a ninety-eight-pound bag of Robin Hood flour, a huge object wrapped in heavy brown paper layed on its side against the wagon. "What a sleep we'll have tonight" was held back by smothered laughs. The front door was opened and since Pa was still working, Ma told the driver the four of us would help her take it upstairs. We struggled with the mattress which wasn't too heavy, but extremely awkward, and finally staggered with it around the curved bannister to the stairs above. Ma ahead directed us where to put it. She could see no heads, just eight feet, so there were no special names called. As if carrying an immense accordion, the leader under the mattress picked out the direction our bedroom was in, and wobbled toward it. Just then Ma gave a big laugh and said, "No not there, it goes in my room." No time to argue, and a little out of breath, we aimed for her room and wiggled out from under the mattress, laying it on the floor. "I'm putting my mattress on your bed," Ma said, as she tugged at the end of our-to-be mattress. "Grab a hold of the end there boys. We will lay it on top of your old mattress." Doing as Ma said, we soon steered it to our room and plunked it on top of ours. Far from disappointed, we prayed for darkness to set in so we could try out our secondhand mattress. In the meantime we went to Ma's room to test the one we thought we were to get. Lying there enjoying the new mattress, our joy was curbed by the thought we'd be losing our cosy snug foot holes. Consulting Ma, we asked slyly if we could put the old mattress on top, trying hard to keep her from knowing our reason. "No dear, no, no, that should be hid, it's a disgrace." So we said a sad goodbye to our foot holes that had kept us so warm for so many frosty nights.

Ours was a high iron bed, three feet from the floor, as boards had been placed on the spring to keep us from falling through. Now with Ma's mattress we were four feet from the floor, quite a spring up when one is praying on one's knees beside the bed and a brother in bed yells, "There's something under the bed!" That's when the Lord's prayer was said in shorthand, as we had just knelt down, only to spring right back up in bed with the rest like we were pole vaulting.

That first night in bed was heaven. We didn't need Pa to order us to bed. We would have been happy to go after lunch. "Look how close we are to the ceiling," was muttered, along with, "It's quite a drop to the floor." We were still in a dream world, and would have loved it if they had even built us up by another mattress high. However two were all we were allowed.

After a few nights of wanting to retire early, a longing feeling returned to our minds which was for Ma to allow us to burrow two holes each, like a mole, in which to place our feet. While we never managed to get our foot holes back, Teedy soon got a foot hole of his own, right through our bedroom window.

When home alone, our gymnastics came to the fore on our double mattress. Our room wasn't finished, so one brother would jump up and hold on to a rafter by his feet. Billy was the one who praised our monkey tactics if we did it perfect, and the only one who had trouble at first was Teedy, as most of his weight was in his head and his rear, and at times we were forced to push him through his act. Billy, always ready with new tricks, called time to run downstairs to see what time it was, coming back up saying, "We have twenty minutes before Pa will arrive, so we'll try this one." Murray, the wiriest of all four, climbed up on the two-by-four directly above the middle of the high bed. He balanced himself sitting on the rafter, while Billy and I used Teedy as the guinea pig, this being a new trick. We had him lock feet with Murray. When he told us he'd got a good clinch, Billy and I let go of Teedy, allowing Murray's dangling, skinny legs to hold chubby Teedy. We then witnessed the fastest accident in the history of the new mattress. The sudden weight of Teedy was too much for Murray's legs and Murray was yanked from his moorings while Teedy took a wall flip, his legs going in all directions, landing side-ways on the floor after one of his swinging, chubby legs busted through a window pane. . . .

There we were, with the smell of Pa in the air, keeping swarms of mosquitoes out with a piece of cheese cloth. The heel impact of Teedy's foot had made a jagged hole which was impossible to sew. We had white faces along with nails bit down to the quick. I knew Teedy was not only down to the quick but was making furious gnaws at his wrists, as he was the guilty one. He should have tucked those roving legs of his close under his rear like a somersault acrobat—then we wouldn't be looking out a painful, paneless window, with the sad old hymn "Nearer My Pa To Thee" on our minds.

Already thousands of immigrant mosquitoes, some carrying small bits of luggage, were soaring through the broken pane. If we could keep Pa from the outside corner of the house, that would be good; and if we could keep him out of our room, upstairs, we'd have it made. But we'd have to move the outhouse, as he'd have to pass our window to go there. And Pa always came into our room to check our suits, to see if they were the way he wanted to see them. If we four could afford a butler to do Pa's job everything would be fine. Or even two butlers, one to be stationed at the head of the stairs with a gun.

Minutes before Pa arrived, Billy found the solution— take the pane right out, every splinter. It looked identical to the clear glass next to it in the same frame. We didn't care how many times Pa went to the outhouse and looked up, he'd never suspect—unless it was windy and the aged curtain blew out. But a twelve-inch piece of string kept it taut to the bedstead, another one of Billy's ideas.

Our goal now was thirty-five cents, which would cover the cost of the pane and putty. The blood we lost during those two weeks, while saving for the glass, was gallons on bad nights. We'd take turns with a newspaper swishing mosquitoes back out while they were on their way in.

Having one hen at the time helped us considerably. She was a good layer, and as soon as she squatted in position to lay, before the egg even dropped to the nest, Teedy had a sale for it—three cents from a sweet lady, Mrs. Boyce, across the road from us. She hardly had to boil it, as it was still warm. Pa wondered what was becoming of the eggs, but we convinced him the hen was moulting, although it was only June. The poor brown hen paid for the window, and as she spit out her twelfth egg, she had a look on her sharp pale beak as if to say, "Now there, fix yer winder."

A good time to fix our window was when Pa was at a union meeting. Careful hands handled the new pane. In a few minutes the glass was fitted, puttied, and then peered through. We even wished Pa were on his hike to the little red outhouse. We were so happy, I think we would have rapped and waved at him.

Back to normal now, the sheepshank knot is taken out of the curtain to allow the curtain to uncrease. And the mosquitos that have marched back and forth over an open border for nearly two weeks suddenly face an iron curtain.

This Cap Will Fit Our Soup Pot

With a good mattress on our bed, Ma's next thoughts turned to clothes for us. Our clothes were well worn. Most new clothing was out of the question. So we were patched, sewn and darned. One pair of woolen socks was bought once a year. They weren't allowed to wear out after our treatment. As soon as a hole showed up in the heel or toe, or elsewhere, it was pounced on with needle and yarn. In time, the whole sock would be darned, giving the sole a spongy feeling when walked on. A disadvantage would be if your rubber boot sprung a leak. When the water seeped through the heavy, darned sole, your troubles started. To dry that part of the sock was almost impossible. With just a coal stove to dry these drenched, heavy fluffers it would take days. But you couldn't leave them hanging on the oven door too long, as they had evaded much washing, and what an odour an unwashed baked sock gives off!

Then Pa would come home with the fall and winter Simpson's catalogue. It was very colourful, with self-addressed envelopes enclosed, along with a budget sheet with enough lines for your order, and some more. Bold letters told you no down payment was needed. To us that was almost as good as saying it was free.

The big book was always held firmly, while many eyes followed each turning page. Everything looked beautiful and cheap. A few questions were asked on the form, which were answered with a few lies to make it attractive, and this was sent back with the order sheet. I was sharpening a pencil stub in the background. A small x was placed by each article ordered. Being a lover of bright colours, a small red cap was to be my limit, not too dear, about eighty-nine cents. The numerous things Ma and the rest were interested in didn't enthuse me in the least, but the red cap glowed in my mind's eye. Getting Ma's attention, I finally got her to turn back to my little red cap.

Reading the small print thoroughly, we saw the first order wasn't to exceed fifty dollars. Chicken feed with no down payment, so my little red cap headed the list. The rest was up to Ma and Pa, and I stepped out of the picture with a warm feeling.

What a lovely sensation going to the post office every day to see if our loot was there. Then came the day I went to the post office and there it was. I could hardly keep from opening the box. Tossing the huge box in my arms I handled it like a shoe box, and headed for the various heads in our window. I was greeted as Santa Claus. Their smiles were getting wider as my grin was getting larger.

The cord was quickly amputated and it's a wonder heads and hands weren't snipped off by the scissors.

In a small corner of the box something crimson caught my eye. But my heavens, what was this, a red manhole cover with a brim? Not wanting to show my embarrassment, I told Ma I had ordered a big one in case my head grew, saying it very fast not giving them the chance to say anything about the size, and holding it with a tuck to make it look smaller.

It was as big as the soup pot that took up four covers on our coal stove. While the rest were tunneling into the box, I walked out of the house so no one could see me. The feeling that had struck me the first time I turned the pages and saw it was quickly fading.

How could I wear a cap the size of our soup pot? That cap wasn't meant for heads. There were such things as tea cosies. Could this be a soup pot cosy? That night I dreamt of people with soup pot heads, topped off with my red cap.

Soon after, Ma noticed I wasn't wearing it and she took an eight-inch tuck in it, forming it to fit my head. I wore it faithfully.

Four days later, wearing the eighty-nine-cent cap, I rushed to the post office again. This time I picked up a letter from Simpsons, saying the first payment was due. Then the struggle started to meet those monthly payments. We couldn't see what we had got for the fifty dollars. The only article we were sure of was the big red soup-pot cosy. But I was beginning to like the red cap all over again, and as it got older, and got caught in a few rainstorms, Ma took out the bulky tuck and put a smaller one, not quite so noticeable. Everywhere I went my red cap was on my head.

One evening, a friend of mine was walking over a high bridge, and looking down from the centre of the bridge he called me over and said, "Andy can you see those little fish down there in the water?" Leaning too far over, off flew my little red cap into the swirling waters. I was spellbound, as the tide slowly took its time and swept my cap out of sight. I only hoped that when it reached its destination it would be retrieved by someone with a head the size of Charlie Brown's, possibly Teedy. Meanwhile, I felt like throwing my friend off the bridge.

Oh, Why Do You Flinch, Billy Boy, Billy Boy?

However much we fought amongst ourselves at home, over money or whatever, any attack upon one of us from an outsider was an attack on all of us, and we were well unionized.

Teedy got into trouble on his way home from school one day. He met a rough character who started giving him a hard time. Teedy could only stand so much of his harrassment. Then he went into his fighting stance, which we always told him to avoid. He charged the bully, head down like a ram, tongue between his teeth. His aggressor surprised him with five quick punches to the face, leaving Teedy with numerous cuts and bruises, and a quite different outlook on life for awhile.

Now Billy was always a wonder man in our mind, someone who could beat anything that ever walked. So we slid along giving guff, knowing we had a big brother that could beat the bully to a pulp. With this in mind, every swing Teedy took from this guy only reinforced the belief that Billy, who could conquer any foe, would get the bully.

Beaten, and knowing he was no match for this giant Teedy drunkenly found his way clear and staggered for home. He laboured himself to the porch and Billy, sickened by the sight of Teedy's face, asked him what had hit him. Secretly, so as not to attract Pa's attention, Teedy led Billy out to the old henhouse to tell him of his experience. "You know the fellow," Teedy says, "the guy that was in jail for stealing and expelled from school for smoking."

Teedy is comforted when Billy says in an angered voice, "Just wait til morning, I'll tear him apart."

Teedy is mothered by the three of us, and eats lightly. His next move is to go to bed to heal his wounds. He disregards all the pain from the licking and falls asleep, secure in the confidence he has in Billy's solemn promise.

Next morning early, Billy escorts Teedy to school to get a smash at the culprit. Murray and I as aides-de-camp follow yards behind. Upon reaching the school, Teedy's monstrous attacker looms up. Billy eyes him and starts flinching, wondering how he is going to get out of it. Teedy, not knowing Billy is slowing his pace, directs him to the laughing bully. We see that the creature is a foot or more taller than Billy and though the weather is in the teens, he is only wearing a short-sleeved sweater and still looks as though he is sweating. Even the heel is off one of his boots making him look a lot tougher.

Billy worms his way toward Teedy's trouble, throws out a few not-too-saucy remarks, and the ruffian straightens up, making himself even tougher and taller, and comes toward Billy. Yeahs and oh yeahs are swapped, with Billy having no intentions in the world of tackling him now, even if he had dis-membered Teedy. Coming close to Billy with thoughts of a fifteen-round match, and with us all ready for the fists to swing, Billy backs up further, delaying his punches. Suddenly the pugilists are inter-rupted by the school bell, which means we have to line up and walk in to the school. Billy's and Teedy's trouble leaves to join the lines.

For many years we teased wonderman Billy that he was "saved by the bell."

Chapter Four

The Seasons Come, The Seasons Go, We Lost Pa's Shovel In The Snow

The Delectable Dump

We lived about a quarter of a mile from the town dump from which Murray erupted. We were blessed to be born so close to a project like this, but it would have been a lot easier for us if Pa had built our house right in the dump.

The dump was at the bottom of a seventy-five-foot cliff. A car or truck would back up to two rails that kept them from going over the edge, and there dispose of their rubbish. We often wished the truck would go over the edge. Then we could have claimed it and taken Pa for a ride. We had a bird's eye view of the dump and so did our poverty-stricken neighbours.

At five a.m. in summer, the dumping started. We called this the sneak attack on the dump, as I think the driver of the wagon was trying to evade us. But one of us four would be up. Then the word would be passed to the remaining half-naked sleepers, who grabbed pants in one hand and boots in the other—the latter needed to prevent slicing a foot or two on broken glass. Half asleep and dressing on the run, we'd scurry down a road that led to the shore, scramble over rocks and boulders, and soon end up underneath the load in close to the cliffs to keep from getting hit with anything but a diamond necklace.

It's not too exciting to get hit with a bag of dead cats —even a bag of live cats wouldn't be much fun, as falling from seventy-five feet, they'd tear you to bits. Once Billy got rung with a stove but came out without a bruise. We always called it the fluke wringer. A couple of us tried to start a fire in Billy, and we wondered how to go about telling Pa Billy had turned into a stove.

While the trash was tumbling down from the top of the cliff, sometimes you'd see something shining in the load, but it would be covered up fast by the steady stream. How fortunate pigs were to have a snout for rooting in instances like this. Our hands just weren't enough to race the greedy bunch to find that object, so we used our feet to burrow through the heap only to find our valuable treasure was nothing but a broken pair of eyeglasses.

You could always tell when they were finished dumping by the sound of the motor starting up again. Then all the pack rats, as high as a dozen, would surge out from under the cliffs to loot. We never paid any attention to brothers or friends, nor did we say excuse me if we stepped on someone's head or ruptured his spleen. The main aim was to look and look fast before the other guy found it—it could mean anything from a toothless comb to a shotgun. During the search, we were never very interested in what the other guy found. We had to spare our eyes to continue that desperate looting. Too bad we couldn't have come across an extra pair of eyes. Only when everything was picked over could we relax and compare prizes, and I'd wonder why all I'd ended up with was a tongue off an old boot and a small box of rusty bobby pins. Why, Pa had just sheared my hair for the summer, so I couldn't even use them.

There would be candies mixed with mothballs and we never knew if we were eating mothballs or round white peppermints. They all went down the hatch. Probably that's why Teedy today has the advantage of mosquitoes being allergic to him and moths despising him.

Once a neighbour darted into the salt water up to her navel to retrieve a floating grapefruit only to find it had the peel side up, all gouged out on the other side. But she decided to take it home anyway. It made a good falsie after it dried and hardened.

One year a new family bought a store in town. Their first move was to clean the store of its contents which had sat on old dusty shelves for about five years. This to us was a most commendable move, although they could have saved us a lot of time had they just come to our house and dumped everything on our front lawn. Instead a truckload full of canned fruit and berries came plummeting over the side of the cliff like small bombs. The impact from the drop damaged some cans considerably. We had been warned that crippled cans could bring on food poisoning or worse, botulism, so we were on the alert to keep away from this disease that only Pa could spell. The ones that were dented were thrown to one side, but were picked up anyway by our neighbours. We took the time to tell them they might be poisonous, but even that was an appetizing word to them. They even grabbed the ones that were bent almost in two.

They trekked happily home carrying hundreds of

misshapen tins and their parents greeted them with open arms. It was the first time all eight kids had different desserts for supper. A new era had begun for them. Why, with all those hundreds of cans, they could have built an addition onto their house.

After these kids took all those damaged tins, we were especially nice to them and would take sneaky looks at their torsos, imagining what a grave future awaited them. We thought they'd die after eating the first ruptured can. But they ended up with more pep, vigour and strength than any of us who chose the air-tight ones, and would usually beat us to the dump after a good meal of that fruit.

At home, breakfast, dinner and supper consisted of peaches. Strangers that visited our house at this time had never seen a family eat so well. Pear, plums, blue-berries also abounded. That season any germs we picked up from the dump were completely wiped from our systems as we were pulsating with vitamin C—and rusty bobby pins. However, I don't think we were too smart feeding Pa so many desserts at once as he would also abound with vitamin C (in fact, he abounded even without it), and all those extra vitamins pumped into him gave him a lot of additional strength when some-thing drastic came up, like us forgetting to clean the outhouse or wearing our Sunday shoes on Thursday. So we studied him thoroughly and when we found him too fiery, we'd cut back on his oats like a mother weans a baby from the breast.

But this fruit certainly came in handy. One day, Murray, noticing at the last minute that he had noth-ing for Pa's lunch can, sliced up a can of small plums, placing them neatly between the bread; and Pa set a record as the first miner to eat a plum sandwich in the bowels of the earth.

Always taught to save, with very little to save from, even the plum stones were put to use. We dried them out, then drilled small holes in them and ran them on a string which Teedy wore around his neck, resembling a gypsy. We could hear him coming many feet away as the stones hit together, making the same noise as Marley's ghost with the chains rattling.

You May Have Pretty Eyes, But It's Pa's Shovel We're After.
Eaton's and Simpson's catalogues should have been off limits for children. No matter what page we turned to we needed everything on it, if not for us, then for Ma and the house. Even in the hospital section I could easily have used a bedpan. With everything from spin tops to corsets, someone was bound to get use out of it. It was torture to turn to the toy page. When the toys weren't coloured, it was bad enough, but when they were coloured, we'd go nutty.

"We'll wait until it storms," was our only consolation. We could earn some extra cash shovelling snow. So we were constantly listening to the radio of the family across the way to warn us of an impending blizzard, or to an old farmer's prediction that if the cows were fidgety or the hens stood at attention with their beaks at a forty-five degree angle, this meant we were in for some snow. The wind would blow up slowly at first from the northeast, directly behind our outhouse, then the snow would begin; and how happy we were to see a fine snow, a sure sign we were in for a good old-fashioned storm.

We would get our poltags (as Ma called the heavy garments we wore in winter) ready for the morning after the storm abated. There would be no school, with all transportation at a standstill. Setting the clock for 5:30 a.m., after wrapping it up in flannel so it wouldn't freeze, we'd hop out of bed at the first vibration. We put on every bit of clothing that was hanging around, right down to a few of our sister's dresses. We'd look quite sexy at that hour of the morning in a bright red dress—only to murder the sexy feeling by putting Pa's pit pants right over the dress, which instantly changed us to hoboes. We looked like plump little lumpy fellows from Mars, hardly able to walk with the bulky clothing that cut off most of our circulation. We had no mitts and that was the main item we needed. So socks that had been disbanded were recycled into mitts by cutting off the ever-so-trodden foot at the ankle and sewing across the opening.

There was no thumbstall and how hard the thumb worked trying to find a room of its own. Actually, the sock-mitts made better pot holders. With four fingers and thumb pressed together, we found it a strenuous job to hold on the sock. But we soon fixed that by sewing two strings on each sock at the top and tying it taut around the wrist, then reinforcing it all with two large safety pins. Have you ever tried to hold a shovel with a thumbless and fingerless home-made mitt? They were no better than flippers.

The people we'd shovel snow for preferred us to bring our own shovels. We only had two, one of which we weren't supposed to use because it was Pa's, so arguments arose in the early morning as to who was to have the shovels. I thought I would fool them by taking the shovel to bed with me that night, but it was hard enough trying to warm six feet, besides mine, let alone trying to warm up a shovel.

While Murray was making the porridge, Billy and I made some molasses-soaked sandwiches, which we found stiffened up like tough pizza after an hour outside. Then the mad rush was on. Teedy had so many

door. Now, to get this shovel first after a storm would be everyone's endeavour. Several times, Billy, by far the slickest of the four, would sneak it up under our bed; and when we had everyone but Pa wondering where it was, Billy would produce it with a gloating smile on his face.

Next door to us lived a quiet man. He had two square-mouthed light shovels in his coal bin. One of us would watch his window, while another tunneled through the snow and gaffled on to them. The kindly man only had one eye, which made it easier for us to take chances. But I guess we would have taken them even if he'd had five eyes. We'd use his shovels for the whole day, leaving him snowed-in to the tops of his windows with nothing to remove the snow but a spoon and a five-stringed broom which we used in summer to sweep our yard. Still, he'd never say a word to Pa, and would always find the two shovels in the same place after we finished.

One storm, our stock market dropped to rock bottom. Geared up for the cold and escorting a shovel under our arm, the four of us headed for town. The family doctor came sliding along in his square sleigh, drawn by a chestnut steed. He slowed, and held the reins while we picked our positions on the runners. If we fell under the doctor's runners and got squashed, at least we were in perfect hands to get immediately glued back together again.

Placing our shovels in the back, we watched the way the snow kicked up in lumps from the horses hooves behind the runners, and we had a lot of fun trying to catch them. After driving us the mile to town, the muskrat-coated doctor pulled his horse in to a small shed. We were eager to start to work after our lift, but when Billy reached for Pa's shovel, it wasn't there. We were almost ready to sue the doctor. But that would do no good, because it had fallen off on the way and we knew it would be picked up by another money searcher. Thus started our day.

There was no such thing as making our usual rounds. We were all responsible for Pa's shovel, even though Billy always claimed it, hiding it from us even on rainy days. We had to get it back, even if we had to call in police dogs. We could have just given them a sniff of Pa's summer underwear, which Billy always wore in the winter, and said, "Now, go find Pa's shovel." But with our luck, they'd probably race off and drag Pa's winter underwear back to us, with Pa in it.

So we arranged our search. Billy and I were to backtrack and look for it, while Teedy and Murray were to circle the town. We closely examined the shovel of everyone we saw. Some people, being complete strangers to us, gave us a "What do you think you're looking at?" stare. We were looking for a small band of black tape near the top of the handle, but it was in a place where the hands would cover it, and this held up our hunt because we'd have to walk right up to people and peer at their shovel handle. Some of them thought we were going to ask them to dance, and even strained into position for a Tennessee Waltz.

The day wore on with no sign of Pa's shovel, and no walkie-talkie to contact the other searchers to see if they had found it. After scrutinizing many shovellers, Billy said to me, "I wonder who is shovelling the doctor's driveway today?" The doctor was his best customer, usually a three-hour job. It was now 3 p.m. With no lunch and tired out, we slumped towards the doctor's. Struggling through the fifteen-foot drifts up to his driveway, we noticed something moving against the huge drift in front of his house. Billy said in a hoarse voice, "Someone is shovelling out my customer and I think he's doing it with Pa's shovel!" Eyeing the tape, Billy's temper flared, as he ran toward this fellow —a real tough guy with one of the worst names in town. I feared all that would be left of Billy would be his thumbless sock mittens. So in case Billy got the worst of it, I stood on guard ready with my shovel. Surprising the interloper, Billy hit him a hard right on the nose, which sent blood flying in spots like little red flowers across the new snow.

Furious punches were swapped, but Billy was very careful not to punch Pa's shovel. Our foe had an outstanding nose and I was hoping that as big as it was, it would start bleeding really hard and scare him into stopping. Sure enough, in a little while, the big fellow backed away, saying he was going to get another guy because it was two against one, even though I never once took a whack at him with my shovel.

As the big guy staggered through the drifts toward the highway, I passed Billy the lost shovel, and both of us proceeded to finish the job the bully had started. We cleared the long driveway and when we'd finished, the doctor's wife told us some rough-looking character had talked her into letting him shovel it. We told her he got tired and let us do the rest, so she gave us a crisp new dollar bill and home we trudged to put our shovels away, especially Pa's.

Without eating ourselves, we went out to find Murray and Teedy. After an hour drifting through mountains of snow we spied our partners, tired out and sitting on their shovels. Tickled that we found Pa's shovel, they then told us they too had had quite a skirmish with a shoveller. Murray said he came across this heavy-set man and thought he had Pa's shovel. He went on to inspect it at close range, almost pushing the man's hand off the handle, when suddenly the man grabbed him by the slack in the back of his pants, and threw him twelve feet into a bank of untouched snow. He thought Murray was going to take a bite out of his shovel. This was the only time Teedy used his shovel all day, as Murray was into snow to his neck and Teedy had to shovel him out without pay.

Luckily, when the man gave Murray that tremendous throw, he landed face-up. Had it been face down he would have suffocated, and with no stretchers around, it would have been quite a lug to cart his remains home to Pa and say, "Here Pa, a man smothered Murray for biting his shovel."

This Free Paper Will Only Cost You A Nickel

Another way of making a few pennies was by selling newspapers. But to get a paper route in the early thirties in our part of the world was as hard as trying to get a job as batman for King George. Only we'd probably have had a better chance getting a job with the King because as you'll soon find out he owed Murray and I quite a sum of money. And it seemed the newsboys in Sydney Mines took on the job for life, retiring at eighty.

One time, to get more customers the paper put on an enormous drive, giving out hundreds of free copies. We were fortunate enough to know the lady who was the head of it, a sweet woman who played the organ in our church. Seeing us with our beloved Pa in church three times a Sunday, she had plenty of time to watch our angelic movements. One cold December day, she phoned to ask us if we would pass out free papers for a month or so. There was plenty of snow and carrying one hundred copies under our arms was quite a load, but it felt light knowing we would receive twenty-five cents a night, so the four of us were over-joyed with our new jobs. Why, for twenty-five cents a night we would have passed out nude photographs of Pa.

Also to promote the paper, the lady gave Billy one hundred Gillette razors, plus blades, to give out to everyone who took a paper. Strangely enough, it was at that exact time when we four, though beardless, started shaving. So Billy never gave a single one out. We took them all home. There were razors everywhere in the house, and we were the only pre-adolescents in North America who shaved twice a day. After supper, we'd take a new razor and unfuzz our cheeks, to beau-tify ourselves for the long road we'd travel that eve-ning to distribute the papers.

Routes were picked out by our employer. She picked Teedy for a desolate route quite far from home in the gang-land section, where his short stubby body with round head would be great bait for kidnappers, though I don't know what good he'd be to them unless they liked the sound of crying. He was good at that. But as he was the youngest, I gave him my route and took his instead. Nobody would kidnap me. I was too skinny. At least with Teedy, they could have taken him home, cooked him, and had a good meal off him.

Starting at five in the evening, we'd walk from house to house trying to avoid dog after dog, a con-stant hazard. We found few people refused the free paper, so with each house we were lessening our load. After the last paper was given away, we went to the lady to receive our twenty-five cents for that day. But somehow this just wasn't enough.

The papers sold for a nickel in the stores and it wasn't long before Billy found a way to make himself some extra nickels. He'd save about twenty-five free copies, take them into town, stand on the corner and call out in a pitiful voice, "Paper, mister?" Many would look through their change and pass him a nickel; and to those who said, "No thanks," Billy would then say, "They're free." They would then make a complete turn, almost breaking a leg, and take one. Surprisingly, though, many paid for them anyway. The rest of us could vouch for that as soon after noting Billy's success, we too were scattered around nightly in different spots in town.

The newspaper lady couldn't stop praising the four great boys she had working so faithfully for her. This continued for a few months until people became familiar with the paper; and it was quite a letdown to us when the free distribution came to an end. We felt we should have been pensioned off. But we enjoyed a fine reputation and we were promised that if there should be any more advertising in the future, we'd be sure to get hired as top peddlers, an honest bunch who distributed the papers as told. . . .

The Letter To The King

Always on the lookout for money from any source, we had heard the grown-ups saying many times that twins born during the First World War years were entitled to receive five hundred dollars from the King. I can't figure the reasoning behind this unless the King was amazed at how two people could be born at the same time during the war without getting shot. Anyway, Murray and I were born a year before the war ended; and though we were never shot, mostly because Pa didn't own a gun, we never received a thing from the King, not even a small crown or a package of Pampers.

After reaching the age of ten, we would put the five-hundred-dollar figure on paper and, adding in the interest, would come up with a very large sum. However, Pa never allowed us to enquire about it to the King. I think Pa was scared the King might get things mixed up, and write back and ask Pa for five hundred dollars. If that had happened, rather than pay the five hundred Pa would have shipped the two of us off to the King c.o.d.

With thoughts of the money plus interest from the King, Murray and I would scan Simpson's catalogue. Price meant nothing to us now. When a brother would say, "Wow, look at this nice scooter for three-ninety-eight," Murray and I would at once subtract that amount from our dream figure, and would shoot a snooty look at the brother as if to say, "That's nothing for us, we're rich, and once we get it, you won't be able to lay your hands on it." The scooter and the other toys never appeared in reality, but the thought of that money waiting for us back in England made us feel like tycoons in front of the rest.

Fifty-eight years later Murray and I are still figuring, but are a little embarrassed to write the Queen now, as I hear she's having a tough time making ends meet. If we approached her with the interest up to date, our figuring would probably wreck her finances to such an extent she'd have to borrow from the Barclay Bank and Lloyds of London to pay off what her grandfather owed us.

But even though the only royalty we had in the family was quickly dissolved in lukewarm water whenever Ma made bread with Royal yeast cakes, we remained on this regal kick for quite a while.

One blustery Sunday after attending church, Billy came up with a grand idea. Thinking again of how we could make a few dollars, and having no faith in our Mayor or his councillors, he decided we should start from the highest peak. We would write to King George V of England for help.

A page or two were torn out of Billy's only scribbler, as we four sat around the square table voicing our wants. Billy had a problem right off saying, "Should we begin with 'Dear King' or be friendlier and say 'Dear George'?" We decided on the latter, and the letter continued. We didn't name everything we needed, but were content with money alone. Teedy leaped to his feet, sputtering to Billy about how he had nearly bit his tongue off one time and could only drink liquids. We decided to leave that out as the King might have sent us only a case of pop and an artificial tongue. Besides, Billy thought that was too personal, and that if the rest of us went on to tell him of all our mishaps, the King would probably have sent us four psychiatrists, duty free.

Instead, Billy began to tell the King a pathetic story about Pa having only two fingers on his right hand and how he found it difficult to work. It wasn't a lie as we four received many a backhander from Pa's crippled right. It seemed to sting worse than if he'd had ten fingers on one hand, as the stubs were rough and bony. Billy decided not to suggest an amount, figuring he'd leave that to the King's discretion, because if he was to put too large an amount down we would appear too greedy.

On the other hand, if he named a small sum, and the King had been planning to send us much more, His Majesty would probably make out the cheque in the amount we put in the letter.

Two pages of complaints came to a loving end, as we wished the King luck on his throne. Billy got us to sign our names beneath "All Our Love", while he spelt out his full name, William James MacDonald. Murray and I decided not to bring up the fact that the King owed us that five hundred plus, as that would have been like biting the hand that was going to feed us.

The deed was done. Now the search was on for an envelope. After a few minutes of looking, Teedy came across not only an envelope but a letter that had been mailed to Pa. The stamp on it had missed the postmaster's mallet by a fly's whisker. Quickly the black-bottomed kettle was set over the coal flame. The stamp on the envelope placed over the spout of the kettle soon came unglued from the steam and rolled off in log fashion. Most of the glue had given way to the steam, so Teedy, always ready in an emergency, rushed for the handleless cup that held molasses and a few crumbs. We should also have mentioned our handleless cups to the King. He might have sent us a Wedgewood tea service.

Billy took over the stamp. Placing the molasses-backed stamp on the right hand corner and at the same time licking his over-dabbed finger, Billy gives a sizeable groan at something he'd just noticed. "We're writing to the King and he's staring at us from the stamp!" It shook us up for a few minutes until the molasses dried; then the King took on a brown look which wasn't as scarey. The dried molasses made him look blind, so he couldn't see us now anyway; and his mouth looked like someone had thrown a gallon of dirty brown paint on him while he was talking.

Any letters to be mailed were put on the small clock shelf, which held the Big Ben. Seldom would the letter be forgotten as it was visible from any part of the kitchen, and possibly from Halifax too. Happy to know the letter was finished, and feeling we four had

had our say, and that within a month we would receive sufficient funds to purchase Cape Breton Island, it was put up on the clock shelf to await next morning when we'd mail it on our way to school.

Pa, arriving home from a neighbour's an hour later, was drawn over to the shelf. Reaching up to pluck the letter down he said, "In the name of God, who is writing to the King?" Huddled together on an old lounge, we never spoke, hoping Pa might think he himself had written to the King, had had a bout of amnesia, and had forgotten about it. Pa opened the letter and read it. "They'd send the four of you to the penitentiary if that letter was mailed," he boomed. And all the time we'd been thinking the King might send us to Buckingham Palace to carry our treasures back in person. This really knocked our high hopes. There were still a few hours of daylight left, but Pa ordered us to bed. If only the King could have seen us now.

Upstairs, stripping our clothes for bed, Billy whispered, "Pa didn't burn the letter. He just crumpled it up and threw it in the coal scuttle, and that stamp wasn't used." We were going to salvage it. Spying Pa making a trip to the outhouse from the upstairs window, Teedy rushed down to the scuttle and muckled onto the stamp and we all felt much better, though it was quite a come down compared to a cheque from the King. But at least we still had his picture.

Later on we got to thinking that Pa had done a good deed by tearing up the letter because the King would have ended up feeling sorrier for Pa than for us, and might have sent him an artificial hand. And after the hammerings we had got from his rough stump, chances weren't too high that we'd survive after he got his new hand working. That's all we needed—a bionic Pa.

104

Finally, giving up on our dreams of receiving money or chests of jewels from Buckingham Palace, we devoted our winter nights, when Pa wasn't around, to filling our stomachs.

The porch built onto the house for storage of kindling and coal was also a good place to keep flour and molasses (also Pa, but he wouldn't stay there). And when the temperature in winter dipped to twenty-five below, I can safely say this eight-by-eight addition was colder than outside—not only butchers had walk-in refrigerators. Our gallon earthenware jug, a sick yellow, was heavy when empty, but with a brimful of molasses it was almost impossible to handle.

After the coast was clear one night, with Pa and Ma out next door, and the old porridge pot soaking on the sideboard, where Murray had made a lumpy evening porridge, we got ready for our special dish—molasses candy. Not knowing how long Ma and Pa would be out, we felt safer by starting the candy making before they had even passed through the small gate to the neighbour's. It took two to master the molasses jug, and it was Murray's and my turn this evening.

A chair was removed to the porch and a small sauce pan placed on the floor. Murray and I wrestled with the big crock, lifting it up onto the chair. Then he and I climbed onto the chair and juggled the jug between us trying to turn it bottoms up, after having had a heck of a time removing the wooden cork. With quite a grip on it at this stage the crucial move was over. We'd heard it said that the higher up you hold a cold, stubborn liquid like molasses, the sooner it will run out. We held it upside down for minutes, not daring to move our feet from the position we'd taken on the chair. It was like trying to balance a meteor above our heads.

No sign of a drop, and much heavier than when we started, I told Murray to get a tight grip while I got down from my perch and proceeded to look up the mouth of the jug. "Nothing in sight yet," I said, poking up one finger. Pulling the finger out roughly, I peeked again and was blinded by a blob of molasses which had chased my finger out. My right eye was totally sightless.

Not caring if Murray had dropped the crock or drowned in the molasses that I had undammed, I rushed to the kitchen to get relief for my suffering eye, shouting, "My God, My God, Murray, I'm blind, I'm blind!" Of all the kids in our family, you'd think one of them could have been an eye doctor.

Out in the porch, the small porridge pot overflowed and all Murray could do was wait for me to help him give the back flip to the heavy jug. But he could wait there until the turn of the century for all I cared. At this moment the top item on my list of priorities was my eye. Why, I'd had it since I was born. I was so busy cleaning up my eye that the time we had saved rushing the chairs and pots around was eaten up by the time we spent getting the stain of a quarter-jug of molasses out of the old cold carpet in the porch. On top of this the coal stove was sluggish and wouldn't heat the porridge pot full of molasses.

It wasn't long before Billy spied our owners coming up the path. As if rehearsed, we all grabbed a spoon, with Murray capturing the warm pot of the liquid, and we scooted upstairs to bed. It never took long for the molasses to cool off in our bedroom since, after the porch, it was the coolest room in the house. Whisperless, we dipped our spoons into the half-cooked candy and soon satisfied our hungry feeling licking up every sup.

Later we smuggled the pot downstairs to its shelf, ready to be used again at four a.m. for Pa's rolled oat mixture, something he had to have eight days a week. Next day, my eye kept sticking shut, and Pa asked me what was the matter. I couldn't very well tell him I had a molasses infection, so I mumbled, "Oh, just a touch of pinkeye, Pa." And after this admission, I was treated to a good dose of sulphur and molasses. I felt like telling Pa I really didn't need the molasses as I'd had my fill the night before.

This molasses candy was quite a habit with us, but we always seemed to get caught in the act, and it was a rare occasion when we were able to eat the concoction after it was fully cooked.

Another night with Ma and Pa only five feet from the house, we didn't even have to whisper to each other what was on our minds. Billy was to throw the ingredients together. I was in charge of the stirring. Teedy greased a large dinner plate, grabbing a piece off a paper bag, coming down on the lard, and spreading it evenly around the plate. We burnt many digit fingers, retaining the blisters on them for days. We'd dip our finger into the hot mix, only to yank it back swiftly and wipe it on our pants (this way, if we got extra hungry during the night, we could always savour our pantleg). You'd think one good burn would teach us, but a few nights later we'd chance dipping the same finger in again.

Four sweet-toothed creatures hovered around the huge coal stove waiting for that dark brown, almost-burnt look, which meant the candy was done. There was always a sentinel watching the path from the neighbour's, in the event of Pa and Ma's unexpected return, similar to awaiting the second coming. As a rule Ma would be well in the lead, knowing we were up to no good and giving us a little time to clear the kitchen. Surprising us this time, Murray saw Pa when he was only yards from the house. Our system worked skillfully without a blunder. Billy with the saucepan, Teedy with the plate, and Murray and I tailing behind, leaped up the stairs and under the covers, staying perfectly quiet for minutes, until Pa got into bed.

A weak seven-and-a-half watt bulb burned all night in the hall outside our bedroom. With the door ajar, a crack of dim light shone on the saucepan, which was still hot in the centre but cooked around the edges. Now we heard Ma checking the stove getting ready to retire. We don't make a peep. Allowing Ma and Pa about twenty minutes to get settled into their nest, all of us huddle around the candy pot on the freezing floor, assured it is time to indulge. Not daring to whisper, as we knew Pa could detect even a change of breath, Billy spoons out the liquid very carefully onto the plate held by Teedy. Murray can't wait so he does the same thing as before, scoops his finger into the blob on the spoon before it reaches the plate. Looks of disgust are displayed by Billy, Teedy and I, but it doesn't affect Murray in the least as the light is too dim for him to see our scowls. For all Murray can see, he might just as well have been eating with three vampires.

Billy has forgotten to get a knife to cut it into squares, so calls to Ma in a very faint voice, "Can I go down and get a drink of water?" With no water upstairs, Ma naturally answers, "OK. But don't forget to turn off the kitchen light when you're finished." Now Billy can kill two birds with one stone. He takes the saucepan back down with him, cleans it out well for Pa's morning porridge; and on his return brings the knife, while the three long-johned hungries are still waiting.

With three ghostly hands held out in the shadows, Billy dishes out equal portions. The empty plate is then pushed under the bed to be sneaked downstairs in the morning. Places in the bed are soon filled, mostly to warm our rears, two at the head and two at the foot. We have only one hand to maneuver with now as the other is sticky from holding the candy. After eating gluttonously, Teedy gets sick and asks us if we want his. We're so filled up by this time, we pray we've got enough room left in our stomachs to lick the remainder off our hand so we can get to sleep. We should have gone in and wiped our hands off on Pa's blankets—for a night filled with fun. Murray complains of a toothache, and the night that took exact timing to execute the eating of the molasses candy is now turning into a bellyful and toothful of sickness. Murray's toothache is stopped by slipping a piece of Pa's chewing tobacco into the cavity, and sad to say the damp chew is not found next morning.

We would usually fall asleep with our tongue on our hand, thinking never again will we eat so much (until the next time of course).

The Sickest Family On Record

During those long winter months, when we weren't corresponding with the King or eating, we found there was no place for us to freely congregate, until we began using the doctor's waiting room. It was a haven for us on cold winter nights and often we were tempted to ask the doctor if we could have parties here too.

A small part of a miner's paycheque went weekly to doctors and hospitals. That amount was a lifesaver for the miners, and also to us for our social gatherings. We felt that since Pa had paid out this sum, we were legally entitled to make use of the doctor's waiting room and occasionally the doctor. The doctors' offices were arranged on the second floor of an apartment building. The main doors faced each other; and each office was surrounded by a large waiting room that contained about twenty chairs. No appointment had to be made. You could go there six times a week, or if you were a hypochondriac, twelve times a week, if you went between two and four p.m. and seven and nine p.m.

Taken care of by a man and his wife, who accepted the job in exchange for free rent, it was always warm there and very tidy, and if there had been any food in the vicinity we probably would have slept there too. These two caretakers were over six feet tall and looked more like a brother and sister than a husband and wife. She had a very raspy voice with an English brogue. At times of emergency if the doctors weren't in that night, when you'd open the door downstairs, you'd hear the gravelly voice, "No doctors in tonight."

On weekends we faithfully went afternoons and evenings, mostly to see the girls. If a girl was stricken with black plague she still had to wait her turn in the outer hall, and we would be there sizing her up and hoping she'd smile at us, even if we ended up catching beri beri. As far as being sick, we rarely were.

Politely, we'd let everyone in ahead of us telling them we weren't in a hurry, and every weekend, rain, wind or sleet, we'd be sitting there on a chair waiting for some sick chick to come in. The caretakers tried their best to put us out, but soon ceased after we kept producing an empty bottle, saying we wanted the doctor to fill it with cough medicine for Pa.

After finishing with a patient, the doctor would open his door, call out "next" and in we'd go. He called us by our first names because we were in there so much and he knew us so well. But we were a lot more interested in his waiting room; and if the man and woman in charge had left us alone, we wouldn't have had to bother the doctor at all. But they were always checking on us, so if we didn't have a bottle we'd go in complaining of a sore throat. It only took seconds for us to get really hoarse and make twitching grabs at our throat while the caretaker was watching. We even fooled the doctor, and when a bottle couldn't be produced we'd show him the sore spot we had picked for the occasion. When he pressed on it, we'd hop half a foot in the air, emitting faint groans. Convinced it must hurt, he'd throw a dozen beady blue pills in a packet and almost push us out. After months of this, the doctor thought we had the sickest family in eastern Canada, a case for the medical journals, and was thinking seriously of sending the lot of us to a health spa in Bavaria to recuperate.

Meanwhile, our house was turning into a pharmacy, and the caretakers began to think we were terminal cases. We prayed for someone to come down with a sore throat so we could use up the pills as big as biscuits. Tablets for blood poisoning were disintegrating in their paper containers on the old cupboard shelf. We hoped Pa would fall asleep on a bed of rusty nails so we could use them on him. Cough medicine that tasted like cascara was downed by us as soon as we got it. One kid who lived close to us, after making numerous trips to the office for cough medicine, was asked by the doctor what she was doing with all the cough medicine, and with no cough—to which she replied, "Ma likes to put it on her pancakes." We had such a steady call for it, the doctor began mixing creosote in it, giving it a grabbing effect on the windpipe. After one teaspoonful, you needed ten minutes to get your breath back to see if you were going to live. We felt like rushing back to the doctor to tell him we were strangling on his cough medicine.

I can see the doctor yet, ladling salve out of a big can, and pushing it into a small rounded tin. We'd tell him it was for Teedy's sore foot (which he hasn't had yet). He never refused us and seemed to have everything we asked for (except food), including bandages and adhesive tape. I guess we did take advantage of him. In fact one time Murray even took in a pint bottle for iodine.

He took Billy's blood pressure once, but after Billy told us what had happened, we never bothered the doctor too much about taking ours. Billy told us he had wrapped a piece of canvas around his arm, and pumped him up until it almost exploded. We steered clear of this free deed, because if our arms exploded we wouldn't have been able to forge our report cards, and would have been forced to write another letter to the King for artificial arms.

One evening sitting in the waiting room for half an hour, Billy and the rest of us were beginning to think the doctor was in his office alone, because no one had entered or come out since we'd arrived. "Take this bottle, it's bigger. Go in, there's no one there," says Murray to Bill. Tossing his cap to Murray, Billy strides into the office to find an elderly woman under the influence of a mild enema meeting his eager gaze. Luckily the doctor is in an adjoining room. Billy backs out quickly, beckoning us to follow him down the steep steps outside before he can tell us what he saw. We flew home with empty bottles that night, with Billy trying to explain to us what an enema bag looked like while he was still running.

One time, Murray went to the hospital after complaining of a sore leg. We went along with him, though we knew better. His aim was for a change of menu and a little sympathy, which he never acquired at home. They kept him ten days and there was always one of us there during his dinner and supper to pick at some of his food. One day some kind-hearted soul gave him half a dozen oranges. Murray thanked him heartily, while minutes later, Billy, just as heartily, took them home to the rest of us.

While Murray was there, he and I visited a doctor's son who was also a patient. We didn't know him very well, but walking past his room, Murray spied a dime under his bed and we were hell-bent on getting it. The squirming and gymnastics we went through almost made us patients for real. The dime had fallen down behind a red hot radiator and should have been retrieved by a fireman with fireproof gloves, but we were going to get it even if our hair went up in flames. Finally we got it, and soon we were the sole owners of two chocolate bars called Three Black Crows. The doctor's son took it all in stride and laughed along with us. He just thought we were trying out some of our famous acrobatics.

The Day Teedy Drowned

After we reached about sixteen, we were through with school, doctor's offices and acrobatics, and were on the lookout for jobs. If only they'd had openings then for acrobatic people, we could have joined the circus. We could have worked under various headings in the circus, labelling us "The Sleeping Beauties" from all the rest we got when Pa was around, or they could have set up a tent for us entitled "Boys who can eat continuously and still be hungry." Then again their flashing lights could have spelled out "Come see the most hideously clothed boys in the world." (Except of course for Billy, who could have been the ringmaster.) Any of these would have been appropriate. But us joining a circus just wouldn't suit Pa. He thought we might be swallowed up by a lion or a bear and ten to one we'd have our good clothes on to boot. And what a loss that would have been, the suits and shoes were practically new. No, Pa would rather we worked in the mine.

Arriving home one cold January night, Pa said he'd heard they were hiring on in the mines in New Waterford and gave us the name of a certain man to see. The four of us got up early next morning and along with a friend we headed across the ice-covered three-mile harbour to Low Point. It was way below zero, and we had on every available piece of clothing we could find, topped off with our eight-foot woolen scarf. Why, if we did get a job, it was going to be quite difficult for us to get around. They'd need a crew there to undress us. When we started out, waddling along like overweight penguins, it was beginning to snow, and before we had gone out very far, the storm was getting worse, cutting visibility to nothing.

Not knowing that the ice cutter had passed through on the way to Sydney Harbour at two a.m. that morning, here it was nine a.m. and we were well on our way across.

It was a blinding storm now, and we were worried about finding our way home. We decided to scuff our feet on the ice, opening a road, so we could follow our tracks on the way back. But as fast as we made the track, it was filled in with the swirling snow. No compass and both sides of the harbour invisible, we could easily have set our course for the open Atlantic, and possibly walked straight to Scotland, where we could have given the King a call to come and pick us up.

Three-quarters of the way across, we came to the channel where the cutter had gone through. Luckily it was about thirty below out here, and a quarter of an inch of scum had formed on the blue water and frozen. Needing that job, we had to make the decision whether to try to make it across or go back. The cutter had cut a ten-foot swath. Getting a good running start we slid across the thin ice one at a time, not breathing to further lighten our body. For all the pounds of clothing we had on, we should have removed everything and slid across nude. Soon the five of us were on the other side of the channel and we continued on to the other side of the harbour. There was still about a half a mile to go by land to the mine in New Waterford; the wind was getting stronger and the storm was getting cruel. Billy, Teedy and our buddy decided to hit back while there were still a few foot tracks to be seen.

Murray and I went on to the mine. "Sorry, no jobs available," was what we were met with, and we lost no time heading back for the shore. We knew the channel would now be covered with snow and would look like the rest of the harbour. Struggling through the storm, we came upon four detective magazines, which Teedy had worn as shin pads when he played hockey. He had told us that morning they fit so well under his wool socks that he was going to wear them all the time for warmth. To the left of the books was a round hole about one foot in circumference, with cold slushy water visible.

Our eyes met. Teedy had drowned.

We didn't stop to study the magazine situation—just thinking: that's the channel, they couldn't see it, and that has to be Teedy who fell in. Murray and I flew on air, like Hovercrafts, across the channel, until we found something else to remind us of Teedy's drowning. There was only one set of foot-prints from there on, and those tracks were two feet apart. The person must have been running to tell of Teedy's death. But where did the other fellow go? Must have taken a different course to the funeral parlour. We weren't long crossing the wide stormy harbour running as fast as overweight penguins could and wondering how to tell Pa that not only did we not get jobs, but that Teedy was somewhere out there in the Atlantic under the ice, with his new gum rubbers on. Arriving home, we hated entering the house, as we could see Pearl looking sadly out the window. When we went inside, she asked us what we didn't want to hear saying, "It's a terrible storm. Where's Teedy?"

Had we been smart, we would have spied Teedy's full outfit hanging on nails, behind the big coal stove— the long johns, three pair of pants, shirt, two dresses, sweater, and countless odd woolen socks. But not noticing this, we went out and undressed in the cold porch, which wasn't as cold as our hearts felt. When we came in the second time, we noticed half a grin on Pearl's face. This sent us searching the house.

We found Teedy in bed at three p.m., and Pa wasn't due home from work until five. Pa was the only one that could get him to bed at that hour. But he soon told us the reason he was there. He had had nothing to change into but a dress, and thought he might run the risk of being attacked by us roving Romeos, so he had retired.

It gave us the jitters as he told us what had happened to him on the ice. Billy and our friend had just barely gotten across the channel. Each time they'd put their foot down, they'd gone through, but as they were travelling so fast their feet were yanked out before the ice broke around them. Teedy was about ten feet behind them (the reason we found only one set of footprints), and hitting a weak spot both his feet went down together. There was no bottom, and he sunk down through the icy water, what he considered about ten feet, before bobbing up to the surface like a buoy. Through sheer luck his arms shot up through the same hole he fell into; and as he was waving them around, one hand clutched a knob of ice that had frozen to the ice. Out he squirmed, sealing himself across to the thicker ice to a spot where he then took the magazines out of his socks, but didn't pause to read them.

Once the wind and snow hit him, his water-soaked clothes were transformed into an icy suit of armour. He had quite a time discarding the waterlogged books, but once he started running he didn't stop until he hit the door of the house. He never even caught a cold and the doctor said that by running like that, with the ice frozen on the outside, it left him warmer than if he'd had on dry clothes.

What In The Name Of Heavens Did You Howl For?

One beautiful spring evening while Ma and Pa were visiting, I was at home alone with our eight-year-old collie dog. There was an old superstition that I really believed and which I wouldn't even argue about today: and that was the saying about the howling dog being a sign that someone has died.

My three brothers were taking advantage of Ma and Pa's absence, and I never had to be told where their hangout was. At times I was a little worried as anything might happen to persons playing on those ice floes at night. It had been dark for a couple of hours and still there was no sign of Teedy, Murray and Billy. I thought about taking the dog, which was sleeping at my feet, and heading for the shore. Suddenly, Prince opened his sleepy eyes, raised his head high and howled in my direction three times. That was all I needed.

Reaching down furiously, I grabbed the dog and placed his body around my shoulders. Holding onto all four paws, I made for the shore, thinking this was all the dog's fault and giving him an odd pinch now and then, rightfully blaming him for the deaths I was to face.

Still holding onto the dog for fear he'd cry again, my blood trembled as I heard a terrible moan, and a large white object whisked past me, almost knocking me over. Nothing could have unclenched the grip I had on Prince now. Knowing this was a single ghost, it meant that only one brother had met his doom. Still a good distance to go, the object appeared again, but this time it gave a crazy high-pitched laugh as it darted by me, and I sputtered as it hit me in the face with a handful of sand. I made for home as fast as I could fly. Now I'd not only have to tell Pa one of the boys drowned— but that he was already a ghost and a stark-raving mad one at that.

Hysterical laughs again. I looked to see the wraith ten feet behind me and gaining fast. Still with an iron grip on the dog, I reached our door and fell in on the floor of the porch. In seconds Murray, Teedy and Billy appear from the direction of the kitchen and ask me why I'm running. The shock of seeing them didn't affect me too much as I was still in shock about what was after me. They were all okay, I could tell by the molasses dribbling down their chin, so that meant that whatever was chasing me was no relation at all. This made it spookier. If you have to be chased by a ghost that's gone bananas, it's much better if it's a kin to you.

After I'd told them what I'd just lived through, they said, "Let's all take a stick and hunt out the ghost." As we weren't too brave around ghosts, we got a few tough neighbours armed with brooms and mops to come with us. As soon as we landed on the cliffs, the vision appeared. Like an army of soldiers, we made for it, but the ghost was fleeter of foot and disappeared into the darkness. While we were chasing after the apparition, a car with lights flickering appeared on the scene, and in front of the headlights we could see two forms, a policeman and a man.

The man was searching for his daughter who had broken out of his house after finding the door ajar. She was insane, and at this time parents, instead of sending them to asylums, would keep them at home if the doors were well braced.

So our ghost hunt was at an end. We walked back home where I ran over to Prince and harshly asked him what he had howled three times for. He looked up with his sad eyes, just a little embarrassed, but with an expression that said, "Well, somebody, somewhere in the world must have died by now."

Leak In Your Eye
Once those long, cold, scarey winters wore out and worries of frozen pipes and cold beds had melted, running into a spring of slush, rain and wet feet gave us the joy of a new, warm beginning in store for us. Looking across the harbour we could see those long, continuous floes of ice cakes, formed at zero temperatures and now honeycombed and streaking toward the huge Atlantic, motored by the high south wind. Those clampers of ice that we'd had so much fun on were now bidding farewell to the houses and small sheds around the harbour.

Useful articles that you'd searched for for months,

without success, after the first snow in November—shovels, clothesprops, and buckets—were now beginning to show up in the yard.

Pains and aches that we had endured all through the winter were now swallowed up with thoughts that it was soon time for Pa to give us a pair of sneakers to relieve us of the heavy gum rubbers that had almost grown to our feet during the cold winter. These sneakers were given to us with the command that they were to be taken off as soon as we came home from school. My how we could run after that change in footwear, and Murray was so fleet footed that he could sometimes fly for at least fifty feet without touching the ground. I myself could jump any reasonable length under six feet, including Pa.

Heavy underwear, which had held our body imprints like plaster of Paris, was now getting its last dousing in the old galvanized washtub. Then we might fall heir to a shirt from an older brother which when new had eight buttons, but when passed on would average about four buttons, two on the cuffs and two on the front. This was scientifically remedied by snipping off the cuff buttons and sewing them on the front. The sleeve situation was also remedied by rolling them up high. An already knotted tie would be added to your shirt, and this took another button's place. As far as ties were concerned, we were loaded with them, having relatives in the States who sent us parcels once a year that seemed to consist of nothing but ties they had purchased in Canada. They were so plentiful that Teedy would frequently change the necktie on the old Big Ben clock that we tied to the bedstead every night so the alarm would wake us with its vibrations.

Spring was in the air and everything was popping,

including us. We were now ready to face the new world, and Pa too, if our braces were buttoned right, with no twists in them.

Something that also came with spring, and something we weren't too ready for, was the rain which came almost every second day. Our flattop house had tar paper in three-foot strips running across the roof. And boy did it leak! While the leaks were in motion, Pa would tickle the roof by sticking straws up the leak holes from the inside so that we could find the leaks after it had stopped raining. Once onto the roof we were to look for all the straws sticking up, pull them out, and plaster the holes with a gummy tar that would harden in time. Pa drilled us constantly about not walking across the roof with our shoes on, as it would puncture the roof and multiply the leaks from previous rain storms.

I was highly in favour of staying away from the roof with or without shoes. The only way I would have enjoyed the roof was if I'd had wings and tail feathers. Not too brave about heights and with a touch of claustrophobia to boot, this one day I was volunteered to climb the sixteen-rung ladder to the top of the roof. Standing on the last rung, I had to make the decision whether to go up onto the roof or freeze and backtrack down the ladder. On a dare I made the mistake of pushing on over the last rung and onto the roof. When I stepped onto the roof I knew I had gone too far. The only way to get down now was to fly, float down by parachute, or else have Pa hire a helicopter to pick me off. I dreaded the thought of going back to the edge. The top of the ladder was only two feet down, but I would have had to roll over on my stomach, hold on good and tight, and feel around with my feet for the top rung. I definitely couldn't make the trip down the ladder even if a forest fire had started on the roof. Had the ladder run up onto the roof, I might have consented, but when you had to dangle over the side and feel around for those rungs why anything could happen if you looked toward the ground. Your head might roll off, or you might take miniature dizzy spells.

Darkness was coming and I'd been up there since eleven a.m. They threw food up to me and it was a good thing it landed near me or I would have starved. They should have climbed up and stuffed me in a gunny sack, like a setting hen, and carried me down the ladder slung over a shoulder. Another brave way to get down would have been to cut a two-by-two opening in the roof. Then I could have greased myself with tar and slithered down into the attic, and from there, heck, it would have been nothing, as we visited that place many times from our bedroom on dull days, eating the old popcorn strings we strung every year on the Christmas tree. However, a hole that size out in the roof would have let in even more rain, and since I would have been the one who had made it, Pa would probably have nailed me over the opening.

In the meantime Teedy, Billy and Murray took turns at the top of the ladder, promising me all kinds of help. But I wouldn't have gone down that way if they had coaxed me with a dozen birthday cakes and a trunk full of presents. I couldn't even look in the direction of the ladder and wished for Christmas to come as I wouldn't have minded going down the chimney with Santa. Finally they gave up and went in the house, leaving me there with the moon and the stars and a bird's-eye view of the whole town.

A small porch joined our house on the western side. One time when Billy was up on the roof he also couldn't bear the thought of going down the ladder, so he had jumped one storey to the porch roof, landing safely on all twos. I thought this over for a while.

Inside the house they suddenly heard a terrific thump and rushed out figuring I had finally fallen off. Instead, I had grabbed my tar can and jumped onto the slanted porch below, the same jump that Billy had taken. Except that the handle had come off the large can of liquid tar on my drop and splashed all over me, dissolving me into a tar baby. All I needed now was a bag of feathers.

My work was now judged by nature. If it rained in a day or so, we'd get the results of my terrifying labours. Pa would never give you any praise when you'd just finished the job. He'd wait for a torrential rain to make his verdict. But I never received any praise once the rain came because what were a few leaks before had now turned into a sieve. One leak caught Pa directly in the eye while he was meditating in bed one morning, and it took about five of us to calm him down as he acted as though a tidal wave had hit the house. Praise be to God we were all blessed with oversized bladders, as all the pots and pans were used up under the leaks. Rooms were almost impossible to walk through due to the different size jugs catching the rain. We should have turned our house into an aquarium. Lying in bed you could name the tune the drops were playing on the tin pans. Leaks that were muffled usually fell on an old winter coat of Pa's hanging in the closet on an S-hook, the kind they hang beef on. That thing would absorb two tons of water before it would drop from the hook it was hanging on.

I wanted to sleep with an umbrella over my head, but Pa wouldn't hear of such a thing, saying it was bad luck. And besides he said I deserved to drown for opening up those new leaks.

If he had known how scared I had been on the flat

roof he would have known why there were so many leaks, because as soon as I got up there my mind was on how I was ever going to get back down. I think I must have emptied the whole bucket of tar on one hole, and by rolling back and forth on the roof, digging my claws in for dear life, I had opened up hundreds of new leaks. At least I knew I'd never be picked for the job, as they'd never get me on the roof again, even if a nudist colony was having a banquet there with an orgy to follow.

Bugaboo

Summertime brought another bugaboo, one which would have played havoc with those nudists. With no screens on the windows and doors, our house was a haven for mosquitoes and flies. (They even had a tennis court set up in our bedroom.) We were told not to leave the windows open on damp nights as that was when brigades of mosquitoes charged into the house in droves to test our blood. They liked Billy's blood the most—he had raspberry-flavoured blood. During these raids Pa would expect us to pass through the door without opening it, like Casper the friendly ghost. Quite advanced in carpentry, Pa made four flyswatters out of the sole of an old boot. This was rough on the flies, with four batters on the swatters, and many times I'd soften my blow, as coming down with the homemade swatter gave me a guilty conscience. Also, you'd end up with a red map of Nova Scotia splattered all over the wall.

But the mosquitoes were much safer. Being smaller they were harder to get, with our ceilings nine feet high and our height five-foot-two-inches—with the swatter fully extended. Then you'd stand on a chair, and even though you never got your prey you'd still leave a dark impression of a half oval on the light ceiling.

One summer evening, with two screenless windows in our bedroom, we had the choice of either dying of suffocation or being aggravated to death and drained by mosquitoes. Those four nude bodies sleeping together in one bed would make any mosquito sharpen its spear and murmur, "Look at this! Wow." With no underwear to penetrate, there was nothing but bare skin to tantalize the demons.

We were never ones to take the name of the Lord in vain, but this morning Billy roused himself and shocked us with an oath, damning the mosquitoes. It surprised us so badly, hearing him cursing, that we were silent for ten minutes without scratching, kind of waiting around for God to electrocute Billy with a bolt of lightning. We were disappointed when nothing happened so the two windows were shut and swatting resumed for hours. But this was merely an act performed by us to entertain the educated mosquitoes who now hid in the cracks of the unfinished room. Murray, who had studied their hideouts and antics thoroughly, could even laugh like a mosquito.

The other thing we had to contend with were flies in the kitchen, and we knew the exact recipe for shoofly pie. Flycatchers strung from the ceiling never helped much, unless you were a ballerina, and as they'd catch around you like a bullwhip you'd have to do a quick pirouette to twist out of it. They were also a nuisance to pull out of their small, green containers. If you got one out without trouble, there were two feet of double-sided sticky paper which lost its grabbing power after drying out in the warm kitchen—also after sticking to your flesh and being pulled off eight hundred times. Then there was a flatheaded tack which was to be pulled out and stuck into the ceiling, leaving the catcher to hang down and get tangled up in your hair. Now I know why Murray and I lost our hair at a young age. We lost it on the flystickers. Being twins and the same height, we were in level contact with the grabber, while the rest got it in the Adam's apple or somewhere else.

Many times Pa would head out for a union meeting, dressed like the King of England, not knowing there was a flycatcher with three hundred and seven flies on it stuck to his coat tail. Unknown to Pa, we'd pull it off as he whisked out the door. Then we'd struggle with it for hours until we were finally able to burn it.

We wished the directions on the flycatcher had read: Pull out flatheaded tack and stick it in your Pa. He would have put up a tremendous struggle at first, but we'd have just shown him the directions. And believe it or not, our Pa would have stuck to the directions better than the flies did to the catcher.

This thumbtack should have been called a foot-tack, because when you tried to thumb it into the ceiling it would drop to the floor to be picked up in the heel of a barefooted searcher. If you didn't lose the tack it was still a tedious job, as that sticky thing would wrap around your head like a serpent, entwine in your hair, flesh and clothing until someone came to your rescue.

Taking one down that was laden with flies and hairs was also a tricky deed. Sometimes by giving a quick tug on it you'd get good results, but then again, by giving it that sharp tug you ran the risk of snapping it in the centre and having the end wrap around your wrist like a boa constrictor.

We soon learned not to hang it over the table or stove because once we had company when one was dangling over the table, and the small tack worked its way out while we were still eating—the catcher falling with the sticky end hitting the open butter dish and the tacky end adorning the company's lemon pie. We were glad in one way as the visitor now couldn't eat the pie. So we'd flick off the part where the catcher landed and eat the rest.

But many a good meal was ruined by some fly that lost its equilibrium and fell into the handleless molasses cup. Spooned under by the last one to use it, the fly's outline was camouflaged, making it look like a large breadcrumb.

One day while hitchhiking, after having covered about eighty miles and walking quite a few of those miles, I was becoming exhausted and hungry as usual. It was getting dark and my next move was to get in off the highway. It wasn't hard to see that the people I picked to ask for refreshment were very poor. But they were generous, as are most poor people. After telling them about my wanderings, one of the women asked me to have supper. They didn't have to twist my wrist. Salt herring and potatoes was on the menu. (The same meal at home made me play sick, but here I acted overjoyed. That was our three-day-a-week dish at home.) After eating salt fish, I always craved something sweet, even a spoonful of sugar. But as sugar was at a premium, there was none to be seen at the table. I was almost ready to go outdoors and graze a bit in the clover.

Under the table was a kind old dog who had a look on his face as though he hated herring, so we had something in common. There were four kind and motherly teenage daughters. After eating those fish, enjoying every bite I took, one girl who must have had the same gastric juices as I did said, "Would you like some molasses?" She seemed embarrassed to ask me, because at that time molasses was considered a poor man's sweet. I replied heartily, "I love molasses." So she went to a little dark pantry and brought out her handleless cup of molasses. She placed it on the table, while the other girls and brother appeared pleased that I'd asked for it. I noticed there were small drippings still on their chin where they'd had it for breakfast.

Setting the molasses beside my plate, she said how good it was for one's health. At this moment I threw my thirty-four-inch chest out, wailing, "We've always used it," and look what a fine sample of physical culture I turned out to be. I helped the situation along further by saying I loved it so much I could almost drink it like tea—a big mistake. Reaching for a slice of bread, I started to spoon the molasses onto my bread and noticed this shiny lump coming up through the molasses. At once I recognized it as a blue-assed fly. Bright blue is attractive to me. I don't know whether the fly's rear was oiled for the occasion or not, but the molasses seemed to be rolling off the fly like oil off a duck's back giving the blue a sky-look, and a surprisingly palatable one. I was almost tempted to eat it, but not quite. Now, to get around this without eating it and not to embarrass these good people was quite a chore. As I was thinking what to do, a cold nose nuzzled my knee. Cutting my bread in half, the big blue-assed fly resting on one half, I waited for my chance. Smoothly I slipped the bread, molasses and fly to the sweet old dog under the table, and he took it as gently as the girl had gotten it from the pantry.

The same molasses cup was on the table for breakfast, minus the fly. One of the girls spoke up and said, "Your favourite syrup is there." I told them I never could eat anything sweet in the early morning. They all seemed to understand as the brother of the family to my left was pouring the molasses on. Throwing a sneaky look at his bread, I saw a big lump in the molasses moving. My eyes followed his mouth and teeth as the strayed lump was thrown in. I slyly cut off my hearing so as not to hear that "plup" sound one hears when biting into an overripe cranberry. Even the dog took on a sickening look as if to say that's what happened to me last night, Sonny, what with you bringing all these flies in here.

Chapter Five

Who's Afraid Of The Big Bad Ghost?

Marley's Ghost

It seems that most of our lives were spent being scared of people. You'd have thought we had enough things to be scared of without inventing new ones. We seemed to thrive on it.

In our front room, the ghost room, stood a large bookcase with two glass doors at the top and two small stubborn doors at the bottom that wouldn't close properly and which would get a well-deserved kick when Pa wasn't around. On the top shelf was a volume of Dickens' *Christmas Carol*. We were never to open these doors, but of course we never heeded these orders once Pa was gone. We knew exactly where this frightening book of ghosts was situated—third book from the left. We could almost pick it out in the dark, but we had no worry of darkness as we made sure that whenever one of us reached for that volume the room was bathed in light, with plenty of onlookers to accompany us.

If by chance I found myself alone in this room, even during the day, though I dreaded to even look in the direction of the old bookcase, my eyes would be drawn to the book and stay glued to it. If you watched it too long, it would open by itself.

With Pa a block from the house, there would be a quick vote from the four of us to go in and look at the picture of ghost Marley on the third page. It would always be a hundred per cent vote. We always had to remember to put the book back exactly the way we found it, knowing how sharp Pa's eyes were in detecting anything out of place. An agreement we made before voting was that no one was to leave the room before the reader, usually Billy, had had time to set it back in its upright position. As Billy told us many times, "If you fellows dare run, I'll throw the book right on the floor." So although we were suffering terrifying thoughts, we had to watch Billy fit the book back in. And only then could the thunderous race out of the room and up the stairs with Marley hot on our heels be made.

We'd follow Billy single file into the scarey front room, as Billy picked his steps slowly, waiting for the three cowardly soldiers behind him. The lights would be turned on and the door to the room closed very softly so as not to disturb the breathless shadows. Then, as though tied together with a rope ready for mountain climbing, the four of us would sidle over to the bookcase and Billy would open the glass door. He would remove the book we had looked at so much to test our bravery. Huddling together, as though in a scrim-up for Rugby, we would form a tight circle so nothing could get in. Billy would turn the pages, passing the ghost page quite fast so as to get to the first chapter. But not quite fast enough, as we three had received a quick impression of the ghost's face. Our blood pressure rose and the hair stood up on the nape of our necks like a dog's.

132

Billy always seemed to have a cold each time he read and this made it spookier. Sounding like a minister at a funeral service the words would pour from his lips. At the same time he'd be watching for a single budge from any of us, ready to fire the book on the floor and then strangle us.

Those first words, "Marley was dead to begin with," chilled our marrow. Then in a deeper voice he would continue, "There was no doubt about that." Billy would pause here to give us a chance to untense our muscles, as he slowly turned to the ghost's picture. Although breathlessly afraid, we were waiting to drink up every angle of the ghost. We had heard it many times before, but the next line could never be finished as by this time we had the full picture in our minds and could stand no more. Still unionized, we gave Billy mere seconds to put the book back, close the bookcase and turn off the light, when away we'd go at high speed.

Many invitations were given to our friends, when Pa was in the mine, to come over to our house to look at Marley. In daytime you felt much braver and volunteered quickly, racing Billy to get the book. With four or more kids there besides us, we'd read further past the part we always use to stop at when we were home alone at night. But even though it was daytime and our friends were all there, if someone jumped and ran we'd be right behind them.

This story was made even more real and horrifying to us because of a small cellar hatch in the room just inches from where Billy used to read. Our eyes would focus on that small hatch as Billy mouthed, "The cellar hatch flew open, and Marley appeared." Wondering how hard a heart could beat before it burst through your chest we looked straight toward the hatch. If it had flown open not one of us would have lived to tell

133

the tale and the book would have had to have been put back over our dead bodies, by Pa.

One night, Billy took the biggest chance of all. He took Marley's book upstairs to our bedroom, opened the book to the ghost, and plopped Teedy's pillow over it. Now this book was never to leave the bookcase at any time.

Murray and I had invented a light in our room the previous day, unbeknownst to Pa, by running an old wire from another room that had a light. The only way to turn our concocted light on without electrocution was with a rubber glove. There were more sparks at the twist of the switch than a burst of fireworks. This new addition to our room gave us the same desired feeling to get up to bed fast, as this was about the time we were presented with Ma's mattress.

Billy had an inkling Teedy couldn't wait for the rest of us to retire so that's why he picked Teedy's pillow, as he was always the sleepiest. Also, he'd been coaxing us to accompany him to bed. Pa was in the kitchen reading his paper.

Billy, with a serious look, had told us so many times that he had seen the book going upstairs once all by itself. We were almost convinced, and Teedy's eyes bulged, knowing it had to be true. Pa had still plenty to read yet, and two crossword puzzles to go. Teedy coaxed us no further, but his thoughts were that he just had to try out the new light. So slipping the old rubber glove on, upstairs he went, turned the switch and marvelled at the display of sparks and sputters the light made.

While Pa was reading, we three were sitting around with a scribbler or book giving Pa the impression we were scholars. Ma was sitting on the old sofa combing her long hair when a sound like a hundred-pound sandbag dropping from the ceiling to the floor caught our attention. All eyes, except Billy's, looked tensely toward Pa. Billy was expecting the worst. The noise was followed by a swishing down the stairs out into the kitchen and, wearing nothing but his shorts, Teedy hopped right up on Ma's lap. It happened so fast we hardly knew it was Teedy, as we hadn't even missed him from the kitchen. He never spoke, just cuddled next to Ma, sucking his thumb, not showing his face, and keeping the secret of his scare from Pa with a few sobs. His actions never surprised us very much, although Murray and I didn't know about the book being up there.

Pa looked over his reading glasses at Ma and said, "We'd better give it some nitre, or it will go out of its mind." While Pa was pouring out ten drops of nitre on a spoon, adding a little sugar, Billy was upstairs getting the book to deliver it back to the bookcase. This was the only time Billy went into that dark room to set the book back in its proper place, alone, which goes to show Billy was more scared of Pa than of the ghost.

Teedy tried to tell us that when he had moved the pillow the book grabbed him and tried to hold him in bed before he made the final leap to the floor. Then something all white had carried him down the fifteen steps. . . .

It was strange that Pa never noticed all the sooty fingerprints on the picture of Marley. There were thumbprints and fingerblobs, and had J. Edgar Hoover been hired to analyze these prints he would have pronounced it an inside job. Maybe Pa didn't notice the fingerprints because he was as scared of Marley as we were.

Radios were on the upswing then, but mostly with

the rich. When their doors were opened and a few strains of music hit the open air we were bug eared at the sound. Talking Ma into buying one was like asking her to buy a fourth car. She'd say, "You know your father doesn't like those noisy boxes, and besides it takes lots of electricity to run them."

One day a neighbour's son, an only child, was presented with one. We were his age and it wasn't long before his mother gave us permission to come over from five-thirty till six p.m. to hear "The Children's Hour." We were in another world while the story was being told of "The Pied Piper." Someone talking and no one there—what an amazing thing. We couldn't wait until five-thirty came so we could hear some new story. Figuring a half hour was too short, we sneakily extended our visit and started coming at five p.m. We tried to tell the neighbour that we were interested in what was on the radio. This was tricky, as at five p.m. they announced a half hour of stock quotations—Alcan opening at eighteen, closing at eighteen. We hated these stock quotations and soon shortened our visits again.

But one day Ma called us aside and gave us the good news, that a salesman friend of hers was putting in a "Rogers Majestic" floor model radio, on trial for two weeks. Christmas was only two weeks away and it made the scene ideal. We hardly spoke all day in case Ma changed her mind. What beautiful sleeps we were having. Every time I closed an eye I could see a radio, and if my brothers had had all their feet in my mouth I wouldn't have complained as long as they left me enough air to drool.

A small red truck pulled up in front of the door one frosty evening. In the back a large square object was covered up by a horse blanket. Two men reached in and gently lifted the radio out. Carrying it through the front door and into the front room, they set it near the old fireplace.

Our Christmas started as of then. This was one of the happiest times of our lives. Pa was still not home from the mine so Ma, accompanied by us, began experiencing this miracle. We learned its off and ons before Pa arrived, and carols filled the room. Beautiful singing flowed from the mahogany box. Then Pa arrives and the off knob is turned. Although never in favour of a radio, he didn't say too much. Nevertheless we weren't allowed to handle it, but, luckily, being born with two outstanding ears each, Pa still couldn't take the privilege of listening away from us.

When he went to bed at eight p.m., the music had to be at nil, but it wasn't long before we found out how to adjust it to a peep. We'd huddle around it with a clean ear next to the voice box.

It was such a marvel getting this radio that we even forgot about Marley's ghost picture in the forbidden book, and at times found ourselves alone in the ghost room, ear pressed to the radio, enjoying even the static.

At nine p.m. the lights were put out, fireplace checked, and Pa's heavy overcoat laid at the bottom of the kitchen door to stop all drafts. I was always the last one in the house to close my eyes. With everyone asleep, I began thinking, "There must be some really nice carols on the radio with Christmas so near." So slinking from bed, over three warm occupied long-johns, I slid quietly to the floor, into my pants, or whoever's I picked in the dark, and felt my way downstairs to the front room. Hardly breathing in case Pa heard me, I adjusted the knobs on the radio. Making sure the volume was shut right down, I was aiming to get a clear Christmas carol, but many stations were storming in on each other. A small draught blew from the chimney and the leftover red coals brightened the room for seconds, only to turn black again once the draught subsided.

Ignorant of the volume's intensity, a sinister voice suddenly boomed across the quiet room, "Marley was dead to begin with. There was no doubt about that." Freezing, numb and unbelieving, I had only seconds to act. Luckily, I turned the right knob for off or I would have scared everyone in Sydney Mines out of their beds. I had fast thoughts of flying up the fireplace chimney, but I might have bumped heads with Santa Claus who was due down this path shortly. Straightening out, I had my gas pedal to the floor as I spun like a car before takeoff, racing noiselessly upstairs and diving into bed with my brothers fully clothed.

A few evenings later, neighbours were in and Ma was showing off her new set. We had just finished listening to a story about Christmas as we were sitting on the old sofa, when the same voice came on and the same words were spoken. Ma allowed us to listen to the full story of Marley; and how brave we were this time, as the neighbour's daughter and mother stayed throughout the story. At this time, nothing could have scared us, especially since the daughter was cute and about our age. Why, if Pa hadn't been there, I would even have crawled into the bookcase where Marley boarded.

Being scared didn't even enter my head, until the neighbours left. Then it was that fast trip from the kitchen to the bed as the sight of Marley's picture in our mind began to torment us again, and like sadists we enjoyed scaring each other. We knew the picture and story so well that we were a little miffed that they had never got our permission to play it on the radio, as we thought we owned the only book.

After my bout with Marley in the radio alone, I was a bit hesitant about going in that room to see Marley. Even today if I was in a room full of people peering at Marley's picture and someone made a sudden move to leave, I'd be well ahead of him, probably even trampling people in my rampage.

However, today, looking at Marley's picture with a group, I would be smart enough to set bear traps all around the room so no one could get out, or else would carry a lasso with me and if anybody tried to get away before me I'd just rope the critters back.

There's A Ghost On My Shoulder

Living with ghosts for so many years, we should have become used to them. But not so. Our house was chock-full of ghosts and they kind of crowded us out.

The only outlet for music of any kind was an old organ we had, handed down from generations of terrible players. It stood in one gloomy corner of the front room. We four boys could pump quite a tune if our feet didn't give out, as they had to be constantly moving to press air from the very weak bellows.

A few weeks after Ma died, on a scorching day in August, Pa was visiting friends and my three brothers and Pearl were on the shore as usual.

Both screenless doors were opened wide to add more light to the darkened front room. Knowing I was all alone, I was building up the nerve to go in and hit off a tune or two. After figuring that I had blinded and aired out those parlour ghosts enough, I proceeded to the old heavy stool in front of the organ. My feet were soon planted on the pedals with legs going full speed as though I was going down hill on a unicycle.

After sweating and working up much pressure, the only song that came to my mind was "Abide with Me", the hymn sung at Ma's funeral. Playing that wasn't too good an idea, but I couldn't stop. It was like diving from a great height and then half way down changing my mind. Why hadn't I picked "The Old Oaken Bucket"? At least I could have thrown water over the ghosts that had settled around me. But no — here I was pounding away at a funeral hymn with at least thirty-five ghosts perched behind me, humming, swaying, breathing, and enjoying the piece I had picked just for them.

In the quiet, empty house the bellows seemed to be feeding plenty of air, making the sound much louder and eerier, and the feeling that swept over me was chilling. I was trying to drown out the ghosts led by Marley who were standing in choir form behind me.

This very sad hymn had no ending because I dared not stop in case those same ghosts that had us go such terrible speeds past the front room door to and from bed were ready to light on my shoulders. Muscles in my legs became cramped, slowing my pace. The old organ began to give off less air. With its weakened toots, giving me more time to think, a feeling of quietness and slow breathing filled the air. Why couldn't I stop and leave the room? Because I knew those unearthly creatures were waiting for just that. No, I would have to play forever, if my legs and the organ would stand up, until I was saved by the four from the shore. Probably they would find me in a heap on the floor, the first person in the world to play himself to death.

In a cold sweat with tingling sensations jumping around my head, I was forced to stop as the bellows finally collapsed. The feeling was as though I had four handcuffs, body-sized, locked around me.

Now there seemed to be a different hush come over the room, much more comforting than I had just lived through after the eighty-six stanzas of that mournful hymn. The room was still very well lit and warm. Everything silent, my flesh was at ease again. Still sitting facing the organ, my feet and hands were still, as I thought of Ma. Spinning the old organ stool very slowly toward the stairs out in the hallway and in not too loud a voice, I said "Ma, if you are in heaven, talk to me." Seconds passed. Then an answer floated down the long stairway, calling me by my full name *Andrewwww*, as Ma always did, only with a long breath as if she was smiling at me and waiting to see the effect it had on me. She didn't have to wait long.

Ma always had a great sense of humour and she had every right to smile now with all the trouble I was having trying to leave that squeaky stool. I seemed to be stuck to the seat and felt terribly heavy as though all the ghosts were pressing down on me really hard. But once my feet did start to move, I must have scattered those ghosts to the four winds, and they must have felt nothing but envy, as fast as they were, with the speed with which I left them and headed for the street.

In the years that followed, I continued to play the organ, but always made sure there was a brother or two sitting in the old rocking chair, listening to my straining tunes—even if I had to pay them or tie them there, because you never knew when I just might slip into my rendition of "When the Roll Is Called Up

Yonder I'll Be There". And if I had ever found myself alone in that room again with that group of ghosts, that's probably where I'd be.

Bring On The Brigade

Pa never made a mistake until the day he set fire to the outhouse. Although we were drilled and schooled by Pa to keep the outhouse immaculate, it seemed he took all the credit for its cleanliness.

Every weekend in the summertime it was to be cleaned and a new container put in. But in the winter sometimes three weeks would pass by before it was changed. So we were prepared for heavy storms. We used galvanized wash tubs to catch the waste. In a large family there's always one or two who get constipated, so that was helpful, as the cleaning would be extended—very helpful on cold wintry days.

Pa's inspection was our worry. Therefore we were hesitant at times to use the outhouse, in case we smudged it a bit. Some distance from the house, it had the same look: flat roof and red shingles with white trim, and a small window in the door as a lookout for intruders—who might at some time have interrupted a secret session, thinking the outhouse to be a Tourist Bureau or a small weighing station.

One cold January morning with heaps of snow hiding the john, Pa rubber-booted his way to the small building which was only showing its ventilator on top, the rest being obscured by the huge drifts. Suspecting that we were getting careless in our cleaning, he proceeded to see if it needed tidying up. He struck a long wooden match on the seat. It broke off and the flame fell through the opening of the seat. In minutes there was an inferno, with smoke bursting out through the looser shingles. Up through the small ventilator in the top of the outhouse poured white smoke, which, if we had lived in Italy, would have meant we had elected a pope. But Pa wasn't even Roman Catholic. Besides I doubt that Italy would have allowed Pa to elect a pope in Sydney Mines, especially in our outhouse.

Though Pa was a heavy man, it didn't slow down his dash for the house, each track a good three feet apart. Bursting into the kitchen, he screeched, "Don't just sit there—the toilet's on fire!"—as though we were the ones who had set it. This news was music to my ears, as I had had the urge to go for an hour or more, but the thought of the coldness had held me back. But now with it on fire I thought I could have had a warm, comfortable sitting.

However, after Pa's hot news item, even though we were all for a new toilet at anytime, everyone leaped to Pa's assistance, grabbing whatever held water, and we all trudged through the tall drifts. Pa was the receiver of the containers of water to quell the fire he had started. We passed him our pails. A small attic in the top which held spare catalogues was crackling happily away when I entered. Looking up at the little compartment, and not realizing Pa was listening, I asked Teedy, "Are you sure all the tenants are out?" Pa gave me a smart smack and screeched, "Go get another bucket of water!" The flames were almost under control, but the smoke was breath cutting. As he slowed down our bucket brigade, Pa thought we should give it another bucketful because of smoking, so with orders for us to keep an eye on it he ploughed his way slowly toward the closed door of our house.

Pa filled his bucket and started back to the privy, when in ran Teedy out of breath with an empty bucket hollering, "It's in flames again," only to run smack into Pa, upsetting every drop of water into Pa's rubber boots. Harsh looks were all he could give Teedy as he dashed to refill at the sink. Then jumping, at times about three feet and still holding onto the water, the rest of us fled to the boonie and dumped the water on all four corners, with Pa taking time to empty the water from his boots before taking that long trek through the patted path to the flaming scene. Very tired now, we studied a new method of putting out the fire by throwing snow on the flames. Pa kept vigil while we transported the snow and it wasn't long before we again had it under control. Too bad we hadn't thought of this first as we wouldn't have scarred up the inside of the toilet so badly, and Pa's boots would have still been dry.

We were happy that it wasn't one of us that had checked the cleaning. Pa acted rather ashamed, which made us feel good, as it was the only time in his life Pa had ever erred. The interior was gutted, but the outside still looked excellent. When we visited this place, looking at the scorched walls and smelling the burnt wood, it added a new interesting dimension, made even better by the fact that Pa was to blame and was suffering pangs of remorse.

Dub Your Uppers

The only time we got back at Pa for all the beatings we received at his hands was at soling time. About once a year our soles were reborn, thanks to Pa.

Our footwear wore out faster than any other part of our clothing, especially in the fall and winter. In the late spring and summer, the soles of our bare feet started to take the wearing. Once we got our shoes, orders came from Pa—no kicking cans or stones, but he didn't say anything about bottles and butter boxes. Out of his sight we'd give a good kick at a wooden box and peel a small piece of leather off the toe cap. This wasn't too hard to fix as we'd tear off the scuff and blacken it up with some shoe polish. Then it wasn't too noticeable to Pa, except when he had the shoe in his hand. At these times he'd have one of us in the other hand. He would talk about the scuffed shoe as though it was a person whose arm we had just cut off at the armpit.

Pa did all the repairing, with the help of the owner of the shoes. He bought the leather from the co-operative in two-foot strips, about a foot wide. It was then our job to soak it overnight in water. This loosened up the stiff hide. It was quite an ordeal helping Pa. Our job wasn't heavy, but it required great skill and precision timing working in conjunction with Pa. It would have been much easier working with God. Surely heavens, He would have had more patience than Pa.

Out in a small woodhouse, Pa sat on an old butter box while I settled not too comfortably on a buckled-up bucket. The little iron last even seemed to bow down to Pa as he twisted it in the right position to work. Sock-footed, and sitting sickly on my bucket, I'd pass Pa the first shoe. Before he placed it on the proper sized end of the last, I knew the next sentence from Pa would be, "They are dubbed to the uppers." I never could decipher what that meant, but it must have been equivalent to lechery. I would accept the devil from Pa for having committed the sin of dubbing my uppers and wonder in silence how in the name of God I was going to refrain from dubbing my uppers the next time.

Laying my shoe on the stretched-out leather, Pa'd outline the sole in pencil and cut around it with what he called the shoe knife which was kept in a leather stall above the door.

My tedious job was about to commence. Placing the cutout sole on the worn sole of my shoe, Pa then opened a box of half-inch small-headed tacks. I was to pass them to him with the head side up, in rapid succession. Two taps of Maxwell Pa's silver hammer, and it was time for another tack. It took many tacks to hold on the leather sole and heel, and Pa was a fast cobbler even though he only had two fingers and a thumb on one hand, which I suppose is better than two thumbs and one finger. (Thank God he never received the artificial hand from the king or I would probably have stuck the tacks into that and been electrocuted.) But to steer that small tack to Pa's thumb and digit finger with the head up was quite a feat.

The first tack was presented correctly. Then the struggling race started. Pa had his reading glasses on and he never missed a tack. This gave me little time to thrust two thick fingers into the small box and come up with the right side. Swiftly, I grabbed one, thrust it at Pa, and jabbed the point into the side of his wrist.

They should have painted the heads of the silver tacks red. This would have helped us a lot, but from a mass of silvery edges it was hard to distinguish the head end. Each time I passed him the wrong end up, he'd start in on me, "Are you that stupid in school?" Now that was one subject I never wanted him to mention, as I had been playing hookey for the past week, and if Pa ever got too personal about school in this small building he would have been able to smell that I was lying. I passed him another tack point first. What I should have done was stay up all night before and press tacks into a bar of P & G soap, heads up, making it much easier on Pa and me, as Pa was in the mood for a world war and I was aging fast and rapidly approaching a nervous breakdown.

It was usually around the twentieth tack-passing that my rhythm would get better. Passing and grabbing were in tune. Then I'd make another slip and jab him again. Then would come another calling down and lecturing. Pa thought this could never be done accidentally.

After the sole and heel were attached to the shoe, I had no trouble passing him the six steel protectors. He placed these gloriously around the sole edge, putting an extra large one on the heel. When the second shoe was finished there was no happier kid in the world. Once I got out of that building filled with the aura of Pa I could let my breath out.

Teedy would be waiting outside ready to go before the firing squad, with a pair of dubbed shoes that resembled two old toads. I whispered to him that I only jabbed Pa five times. I felt free now and as I thrust my heavily protected shoes one ahead of the other, I'd hear from the woodshed behind me, "Are you that stupid in school?" then a few seconds later an, "Ouch" as Pa received another of many jabs from Teedy.

Teedy, hoping Pa would run out of nails, was less fortunate than me. Not only did he jab Pa more, but in the middle of the soling he knocked over the small box of nails and half of them went through a crack in the floor. Pa's holler to us had the same effect as a police whistle and we three appeared on the scene in seconds, thinking Pa must have missed a nail and conked Teedy on the head instead, wanting us to revive him. But we soon found out about the lost nails and what our job was to be.

The small shed was pried up, then blocked up to a height where someone could crawl under. Teedy stayed with Pa while we jacked up the building. And we wished we could have kept racking it up to about ninety feet, so we wouldn't have been able to hear Pa giving Teedy hell. Soon Murray scrambled underneath and unearthed the nails, passing us a quick few in case Teedy was standing idly by waiting for more when Pa ran out.

Pa's orders were to take out the timber and let it down. Like experienced contractors, two pried at the woodshed while one hammered the blocks out with Pa's special axe. Soon the shed was level again and the blocks put back in the old hen house.

Then the door of the shed opened and Teedy stepped out with a shoe in each hand and a quarter of a smile as though he'd just been released from Sing Sing after serving a few years. We all congratulated him as the first person to complete the soling of a pair of shoes in midair. Shortly after, Pa, the warden, appeared, asking us if we put the blocks and the axe back. Three "yes sirs" answered his question, but seconds later, in shocked amazement, remembering his last words, "axe back", we realized the axe was still under the shed.

Pa advanced to the house with the hammer to place it on its nail, where he wanted to see it at all times. In the corner of the shed, not facing Pa's window, an urgent discussion was in progress, each one of us blaming the other for being so stupid. Darkness descending was a Godsend for us as Pa wouldn't ask for the axe now unless he was planning to get rid of our only hen that furnished him with an egg daily for his lunch can, or unless he had plans to become an axe-murderer that evening.

So when Pa went to the mine next morning the barn raisers were at it again, and for the second time in twenty-four hours we hoisted our small shed in the direction of the heavens, as Teedy bent down in his newly soled shoes to retrieve Pa's special axe. To anyone in the vicinity who had been studying our actions for the past day, it must have appeared as though we had murdered someone and had thrown them under the shed, along with the murder weapon, and that we were planning to murder again by retrieving our weapon. Or they might have just thought this was a pagan ritual we performed twice a day to enlist the gods help against Pa's wrath at soling time.

Playful Pa

Even when it wasn't soling time, Pa always seemed to be loaded with wrath. I think he bought it by the barrelful at the co-op. It was very rare to see Pa in a jolly mood. I can truthfully say it happened only twice in our lifetime. At such times he would become as playful as a kitten with a ball of yarn. This was actually very hard on our nerves, because then it was up to us to see to it that Pa kept this joyousness at a fever pitch. It was kind of like trying to keep a grizzly bear constantly chuckling. Sooner or later, it had to come to an end, as do all good things. But with Pa in this million-dollar mood things usually always came to an end before they even started. We would do nothing to hamper Pa's merriment if we could possibly help it, even if it meant glueing our mouths shut so we wouldn't hurt Pa's eardrums with our loud voices and spoil his good humour.

During one of these rare moods of playfulness, Pa got down on all fours and pretended he was a horse. Then he took us one by one on a short ride across the kitchen and back, where he backed up to a chair so we could dismount and another brother take his turn.

By this time all of us were laughing hysterically with Pa. Two thirds of the laughter was to build up Pa's good spirits, the other third was because Pa looked so foolish and so out of place whinnying there on the floor. The small kitchen was ringing with this phony laughter as it came my turn to hop aboard dear old funny Pa. Thinking, "I'm going to make this a good one," I took a gigantic leap from the chair, as a fake laugh gurgled from my throat. At the end of my gurgle, I noticed poor old Dobbins' four legs had given away and Pa sank to the floor with a groan.

As Pa's groans and doubling up increased, I decided it was no fun there anymore as my horse was useless, and I slid to the floor wondering if it was possible that Pa was about to give birth to a colt. Slowly, Pa got to his feet. There was a noticeable change in his complexion and he pointed a fiery finger at me and declared, "You busted my boil." He then blustered on, "You fellows jumped around enough for tonight. Now get to bed." My brothers glared at me in disgust, whispering that I had spoiled Pa's fun and ended the party, asking me why I had to take such a furious leap. But I had just been trying to make conditions even happier for Pa. Why if I had known he was sporting a blind boil on his rear, heaven knows I'd have clung to his front quarters, and possibly lopped off one of his ears.

After that, whenever I saw Pa feeling his oats or in a gay mood to play steed, I would go along with the rest, but a lot more subdued than before, as my poor animal might again be afflicted with boils and I'd cripple him for months.

It always seemed that no matter how carefully we planned things to get Pa up to this high note of playfulness, something always happened to send him to the bottom of the scale, and it was always my fault.

Whether Pa was coming in or going out of menopause, I'll never know, but for the second time in his life he was in a jovial mood. Two brothers were playing forty-fives at the time when playful Pa suggested we all play. This was all we needed to ruin the night. It was rough having Pa against you, but rougher still if he were with you, because if you hadn't played your hand right it would knock him right out of his jolly mood. Then again, if Pa were against you, you wouldn't be too brave nailing his jack with your five, so you'd hold back as though you were dumb. To keep Pa giggling in his strange mood we let many a good one pass that we could have flattened.

Just after supper, we had all been playing car with our truck rims and car rims, which Pa had told us a million times to get rid of. We treasured these rims and sandpapered the rust from them to make them look trim. Then down the road we'd whirl pushing these rims with high thoughts of Cadillacs and Lincolns on our minds. Pa never wanted them near our yard and warned us to keep them outside in a vacant field. During the day, we four would line up in single file and glide our rims over a road we had patted down with new sand. Making those rim marks in the sand gave us that extra added feeling that we were driving a car. Each of us had his first initial engraved somewhere on his rim, scraped on with a dull chisel. And we would never lend our wheels, even to a brother.

For supper this night, we had had prunes for dessert, and it was now about 10 p.m. and Pa's were nearly digested. We were all in our bare feet this warm summer's evening, even Pa, as he suddenly held up our hilarious card game. Smiling, he said he had to take a short trip to the toilet. We all tried to hold on to our hypocritical laughter until Pa had finished his mission.

Soon we heard agonizing moans coming from

around the corner of the house. Jumping up from the table, we muttered, "It can't be Pa. He's out in the toilet." And prunes couldn't have put him in that much agony. Then we saw him staggering out of the darkness, holding onto his knee, which was bleeding like Niagara Falls. We were all wondering what had happened to dear Pa, when he clarified the situation by letting out a screech saying, "What did I tell you about those rims?" Unfortunately, our happy card-shark of a Pa had stomped on a rim while it was laying flat, and the weight of his two-hundred-and-fifty-pound body had flipped the rim up at supersonic speed, belting him about a quarter inch above the kneecap.

All cards evaporated from the table as Pa surveyed his injury under the light in the kitchen. With enough energy in him to ask whose rim it was, I knew without anyone detecting the initials that it was mine, because I remembered the prunes had struck me too while I was joyriding with my rim after supper, and my parking place had been close to the toilet. Afterwards I had felt so good I had forgotten to put my wheel in the field with the rest of them.

I don't know whether Pa thought he'd bleed to death in front of his sons or what, but his temper seemed to be weakening, possibly from the loss of blood. Everything pointed to a tourniquet as we patted the cut with flour to stop Pa's bleeding. Heroically, I presented Pa with the only shirt I had as Billy performed the tourniquet he had learned in his two sessions of attending scouts.

The bleeding came to a halt, and I don't know if we were glad or sorry when Pa finally came back to his old self again. He launched into a fit of rage and ordered the four of us to run our rims over the cliff, two hundred feet from the house. I can still see my rim, which had attacked Pa, as it sped on and on, then took that final downward leap one hundred feet to the water below, followed by Teedy, Murray, and Billy's Cadillacs.

So as you can see, it never paid to be friendly with Pa, to chime in with his wit and good humour, as the devil was always lurking somewhere in the ditch waiting for a chance to change Pa back to Pa.

What A Way To Go

Another time Pa was rather active, though completely devoid of good humour, was the time he decided to gyprock the boys' room. Whenever we had company, Pa would shut the four of us in a little room the size of a closet and forget about us. Then he would sleep peacefully, not worrying about us being bundled up almost on top of each other. We were given all kinds of warnings not to make noise, no matter if a brother had five toes sticking up your nose.

This was the situation we had to comply with when company was staying overnight. But we still loved to see them come because this meant a change in dessert for us, also a little better temperament from Pa. The company of course never realized they were stepping into our room and shoving us out like packed sardines, because we'd given them such a sincere grin to welcome them.

Pa felt a little embarrassed about the condition of the room the company had to sleep in. He should have let them sleep in the closet where we were. Then he wouldn't have had to worry about them seeing the condition of the room as they would have smothered as soon as he closed the door.

Then Pa came up with the fruitful idea that he and

the Bunny Rabbit woman, a Newfoundland lady who at times was our housekeeper after Ma died, should gyprock the room and put a light in it. So Pa gave Bunny orders to phone the local lumber company for the amount needed. We were really happy about it, even though we knew that when overnight visitors came we would end up in our claustrophobic compartment, with the torture of flying feet, rears unlimited, and the condensation from everyone's breath filling the room. Cramped up all night long in those tight quarters squashed us up into grotesque forms. But next morning, minutes after we'd squeezed out, we'd slowly begin to take on our own human forms again, like beachballs being inflated.

Soon the stage was set for the carpenter and carpentress, and I won the official job as nail passer. Pa was under great strain holding a four-by-eight piece of gyprock in place, and sometimes I'd pass him the nail point end first, like with the shoe soling. I soon turned it head first, after getting hell from Pa, who was working without his glasses and had hammered the pointed end.

Bunny was at one end measuring, and her first measurements were off only by six inches. But soon after Pa's shouts and orders, she turned into a first-class measurer and volunteered to pay Pa in cold cash for the blunder she had made previously. Pa accepted as the building continued.

The walls were first, and everything was going along well, except for Bunny's six-inch mistake. I could hardly wait for the ceiling to be started. Terrific measurements were metered out by the rabbit woman, who became sole owner of the tape, and Pa was arriving at the stage where he'd have trusted her with measurements for the queen's lavatory. I think it

154

must have been the altitude affecting him. For extra added height to reach the nine-foot ceiling, Pa stood on a small egg crate. We could see Miss Bunny was also getting very confident, and each time she'd flash the tape out with a dramatic flourish.

The first sheet that went up on the ceiling made such a change in the appearance of the room that if it had been up to me, I'd have stopped the remodelling then and there. But there were five more sheets to go. Pa, not being much of a carpenter when he built the house, found that the floor had a thirty-degree slant, and as he worked his way across the floor the egg crate was getting shorter. Pa used a T-board to hold the gyprock in place until it was nailed.

Pa, standing on the crate with his two-hundred-and-fifty-pound frame stretching his five-foot-eight-inch height to its utmost, hollers to Bunny, "I'm still three inches from the ceiling." Miss Rabbit, having majored in measurements for the last few days and thinking Pa is depending on her for the three-inch raise, smiles as though to say, "Don't worry. I'll think of something. Three inches more. Hmmmm." Bunny's mind is racing. Pa is almost breathless. Then Bunny spies an Eaton's catalogue, with a neat three inches of advertising. She rushes to the old bookcase and back to Pa, who is now panting from holding the gyprock up with the T-board. His glazed eyes look as though he will accept any offer to heighten his reach. Bunny, who seldom does anything Pa approves of in the way of house-keeping, runs toward Pa's poised frame and gives an authoritative command for Pa to jump, so she can squeeze the catalogue under his feet while he is in orbit.

At this torturous moment, Pa would have agreed to buy Bunny a fur Cadillac. With everything hanging in the balance, up into the air Pa leaps, as though springing from a trampoline. The catalogue gains only a little entrance, while Pa forgets the responsibility of holding up the sheet. Everything, including Pa, lands on the floor in a heap, the sheet of gyprock in six pieces. Minutes pass in silence with all eyes on Pa, and Bunny knows she has lost all priority. When Pa comes to we expect him to give Bunny the loud order that he so often gave to us of "Go to bed". Instead he cools his temper considerably by the calling down he gives her for ever suggesting such a foolish idea. Remembering his flight through space, I am thinking, "My, what an athletic, astronautical Pa we have."

After that the ceiling was never finished and remained four sheets short. When it rained really hard on the flat-roofed house, we'd switch our bed around so we were directly under the gyprock, and it was good looking at something other than nail bottoms. We were glad Pa had called a halt to the renovations as the partially-finished ceiling gave us the perfect compartment in which to hide cigarettes if we poked them in far enough. Pa's arms weren't as long as ours. As for the company who may not have liked the look of the ceiling, we thought it might have been a good idea to present each of them with a pair of blinders that horses wear, so that they'd only be able to see the finished part.

Chapter Six

Growing Up The Hard Way

I Didn't Know There Were Angels In Halifax

In the fall, especially after Ma died, it was pretty dreary in Sydney Mines. There was no work, no recreation—just day school, which to me was like day prison. There was something about the fall that brought out the joining instinct in us, though we never seemed to last long—like when we joined the boy scouts and were thrown out after accidentally bashing the scout master's skeleton into a hundred pieces. But we would have joined a nunnery to get away from Pa. Pa would have us preparing for winter ahead by gathering wood and coal from the shores—anything that would burn in our coal stove.

Billy came home one evening with the gracious news that an organization known as the Band of Hope was to assemble in the old Orange Hall every Friday evening throughout the fall and winter months, from seven to nine p.m.

What a release that would be from Pa, and better still it was on a Friday evening—meaning no school next day. We were very excited, but showed no emotion, until Billy had had a chance to transmit the news to Pa. Billy was extra slick at conning Pa and would spring things on him while ironing a pile of his shirts or shining his shoes. Although we'd been barred from scouts, and almost from church and school, Pa still thought we were actively affiliated with them and acted sort of proud when friends would bring up these groups in conversation.

Now we were ready to embark on another *Named Gathering*, and we were wondering how slippery Billy would approach Pa—as we needed Pa's OK to wear our Sunday clothes on that blessed night.

Pa loved all kinds of reading material. Billy had a friend who read western magazines weekly, and he'd save them for Billy. So he waited until he got six from his friend and then used them to bait Pa with, before he asked any questions. After greeting Pa at the proper temperature, he came out to us smiling, saying, "I've known your father longer than you, and he said you could join." We didn't know who we felt like kissing, Billy or Pa. On Tuesday we were wishing the world would forget about Wednesday and Thursday, as Friday was the only day we were now living for.

When that day came, it was made even better because Pa was selected for a union meeting that night. So here we were putting on our choicest clothes, going to a place that was inhabited by girls, and to top it all off—refreshments at the end of the meeting. Murray and I looked so gorgeous after we were dressed that we gazed at ourselves in the kitchen mirror for at least an hour, twisting our faces and smiling in different ways preparing for the sweet, loving chicks we'd see at the meeting, at which point we would engulf them with our favourite smiles. Had we known Pa wouldn't be home before us, Murray and I would have carried the mirror to the hall with us.

The four of us were soon dressed like actors and we

walked towards the hall as though total strangers to one another. Each one thought he was the best looking, so no word was spoken as we climbed the twenty steps to the second floor, settling fast in the best-lit seats which contained many girls and boys who had gotten there earlier, because they never took the time we did to aggravate the mirror.

On one side were over a hundred girls and directly across from them in as many seats were the same number of boys. We began casing the joint, along with the girls who were tittering inside their hands. We were glad we had practised our glances and facial movements in the mirror, as across the aisle there were at least four girls looking in our direction. If Pa had said, "Do you take her to be your lawful wedded wife?" we'd have answered, "Yes, Pa, we truthfully adore them all."

The evening was wearing on as the small platform in the centre was filled with two women and three men, who were the instigators of the Lodge. A pound of the gavel—the first one most of us had seen—brought the meeting to order, with us thinking the gavel would be ideal for cracking nuts at Christmas, or Pa's head anytime. As usual there was the same bally-hash you hear at all openings of meetings—about order, please listen, etc. Then we were to all stand and repeat the pledge: "I promise to pledge myself from the use of tobacco in any form, and from bad language. Look not upon the wine, when it is red, when it giveth its colour in the cup (we never got a chance to see its colour in the cup—we drank it from the bottle), for at last it biteth like a serpent and stingeth like an adder." (Here I think they were talking about Pa if he had caught us drinking the wine.) The leaders continued on telling us what was right and what was wrong. We were always interested in what was wrong, and listened attentively to see if they named a few things we hadn't tried yet.

Billy was the most distinguished-looking fake in the whole bunch, though his attire consisted of Pa's best pants with a belt tied in a knot around his chest to hold them up and our young sister Pearl's woolen sweater for underwear. He wore Pa's railroad watch, which Pa forbid us to even look at. But here was our Billy with the chain running around his chest like an iced snake in the circus. It certainly added to the charm he bestowed on the dentist's pretty daughter, along with the lawyer's blonde offspring. Both had had their eyes glued on Billy as soon as he entered the hall. Very few stared at me, and at times I thought I should sit on Billy's lap and then we could have whispered to each other about who we thought they loved, him or me. But after thinking it over, I figured I'd look kind of fruity sitting on Billy's lap the first night, when I was nearly as old as he was.

The first half hour was spent in forming a committee of young kids—president, secretary and treasurer—elected by the majority of hands raised. The office of president was at stake. Sitting beside Billy, I was shocked for minutes when a sweet little cross-eyed girl directly across from Billy and I pointed her polished nail right at me, and in a soft silky voice said, "Him, him." Blushing and flushing, I was flabbergasted. Now I knew how Roosevelt felt when he was elected president. Her nomination was accepted and she was told to walk across and touch the one she had so quickly nominated. Forgetting about Billy next to me, I tried to untense the shoulder I knew she'd touch when she walked over to me. Desperately attempting to relax for her nudge, I saw her small frame walk in my direction, then two feet from me she steered her body away from me and touched brother Billy on his shiny shoulder though still looking me in the eye.

I was happy they couldn't read my mind and I gave a sickly laugh as Billy arose and took his seat as president while the hall was noisy with applause. There were other seats left. Maybe I'd be voted in as janitor if there was such an office.

Billy was loved even more by the girls as he settled himself into the president's chair, shuffling his body around like a hen on too many eggs. I slumped down in my chair with thoughts of, "What's the use."

Teedy and Murray on my far left looked the same as when they had left home, sexy and masculine, even though they had won no offices either. But one out of four wasn't bad, so we took advantage of Billy's authority. Billy was handed the gavel, after being told when to use it. He called the meeting to order with a light tap on the hardwood desk. Making use of our rights with Billy the Master, we continued to talk. Then Billy gave a much louder thump, looking in our direction, and knowing Billy as we did, we were quiet, as Billy would have aimed for our temple with the wooden mallet, and we knew he wouldn't miss.

Then a little man stepped up to the platform, sputtering and fuming so that we had a hard time understanding what he was saying, and told us we were to be visited by an archangel from Halifax. Then we were told by some other adults how we were to behave and so forth, as this was to be our first test before an archangel. Now we never asked any questions as the meeting was being adjourned and refreshments came next, but it left most of us puzzling over what an archangel was. Could it fly? Why, we never dreamed there were angels in Halifax. Maybe he was going to float into Sydney Harbour in Noah's ark, and then take an angelic swoop over to the hall for the meeting. We wondered whether we should take Pa's scoop net the following Friday to catch that thing so we would become heroes in front of the girls. But it might have taken a flap up into the rafters and perched there with its harp.

To tell you the truth it was a bit nerve-wracking looking forward to the arrival of an angel. We'd never known anyone who had met an angel before. Did you shake its hand or pump its wing up and down?

The remainder of the evening, girls shook hands with Billy, wishing him the best, and I wished I could have been one of his hands. Instead I sat there, sweating and trying my best to control my eyebrow shadow, but the only stares I was getting were from Murray and Teedy. I yawned and said, "I thought they were going to have something to eat."

Billy made Pa feel like a father who had just got the news his son had been elected prime minister of the world as he showed him his presidential papers. That opened a fine path for us, as we could tell what Pa was thinking: "They'll learn something there. I can feel it in my bones." Pa was so mesmerized and mixed up, I think we could have worn our Sunday clothes on Monday.

It wasn't long before the Friday of the angel rolled around. Pa was home this time while we were dressing, so we didn't have that same masculine feeling as we had had last week when he was out. We dressed in secret and sneaked past Pa as he smoked his pipe on the old rocker. We wore our caps, which we hated, but we couldn't chance taking Pa's scoop net with Pa sitting watching us. We figured if the old archangel got too rambunctious, the four of us could slap it down with our caps, assuming it was no bigger than a bird.

Pa would be proud of us then. We'd be the only family to capture an angel.

The crowd was assembling fast. Excitement filled the hall. There will soon be an angel in Sydney Mines. Teedy, Murray and I almost followed Billy to his high seat, until he shooed us back to sit with the rest. The meeting was opened by Billy as he read the small paper in front of him. In a hypocritical voice Billy reeled off, "The archangel will be here in a few minutes, so everyone remember what manners to use." I hadn't been as excited since Pa tramped on the tire rim and nearly amputated his leg.

The door opened and something not-too-tall with a slight limp padded in with red banners (these must be his wings) streaming over his shoulders. Had we the oil shortage that we have today, I would have sworn it was an Arab trying to sell us some cheap oil. Billy stood, as did the others who held offices, seating himself after the "whatever" was seated. So that was an archangel. Why he never even brought his harp. However we were glad to see he was only about the size of a puffin, so if he took to flapping around we could catch him easily with our caps.

The archangel had a look on his face as if he would burst out crying. Every paper he pulled out of his pocket was a pledge, the same as before, one from smoking, one from drinking, and we were praying there wasn't one from women. He read them aloud so they would sink in, but we knew Billy had half a cigarette in his back pocket, and no archangel was going to confiscate the president's cigarette, not while we three were promised some of it after the meeting.

To make the archangel feel at home, cake, cookies and sandwiches were brought in by the elders. How proud Murray and I were to be picked by the head

163

matron to go downstairs to the cold kitchen to warm up a huge potful of cold tea, already steeped with milk added. Imagine, we were going to supply liquid for an angel. We didn't even think angels cared for such material things as food and drink. As Murray and I were about to leave, a rough character asked if he should go also and got an affirmative nod from the matron.

The big pot held about five gallons of cold tea, and the coal stove's covers were brown from no fire in it for months. Kindling was picked up here and there, and it was a muggy night so it was slow to burn. They should have asked the angel to perform a miracle and heat the tea.

A big mistake they made up above was to pass out the sandwiches and cake a few minutes after we went down to heat the tea. So they were now at the choking stage with all that dry food—especially the archangel, who had used up most of his saliva nibbling and telling yarns.

A call from the matron at the top of the stairs inquires if the tea's hot yet. "In a few minutes," was our reply, but it wasn't even warm, as the kindling was damp. During the wait for the fire to burn, we were searching the cupboards. Murray found a large box of pepper, and we knew this was hot. In goes the full package, which was stirred around quickly by the kid she had sent with us, who was a ten-year-old gangster in real life.

When the anxious voice called again, there was nothing to say but, "Coming." Ice cold, but red hot, the liquid was transported upstairs with Murray and I holding the handle, our helpmate leading and opening the doors for us. Poured from the huge pot to gallon pitchers, the tea was passed around to a dry-throated crowd who hadn't a crumb left of anything to eat with it. It looked like great tea, though no clouds of steam arose. But they had asked for it.

It was only proper that the archangel's was the first cup poured, and only logical that he was the first to choke gaspingly, while in the midst of an interesting tale. First he closed up like a clam, then went into a spasm of strangled coughing. Had he taken a small sip, he could have controlled his seizure. But the extra big gulp he took cut off his breathing and left him coughing like one who had smoked twenty packs of cigarettes a day for the last eighty years.

Small coughs were erupting all over the hall. At first the matron thought everyone was trying to imitate the archangel just be be friendly. Soon she smelt a rat. She went downstairs, found the empty pepper package, and looked at us with horror in her eyes. Murray and I and our gangster friend were ordered not to come back. I guess this meant we hadn't passed the archangel's test. And while we didn't care if he told God about us when he fluttered back to heaven, we certainly hoped he didn't tell Pa.

Murray was disgusted he hadn't grabbed a few sandwiches before we went down to heat the tea, as the whole thing was kind of a letdown. However, we stayed long enough to see Billy close the meeting, knowing he and Teedy would join us. The matron, with the help of Billy and the secretary, was placing the long robe over the archangel's shoulders, as he was still smothering a few coughs with a "this-is-the-last-trip-to-this-joint-for-me" look on his face. Escorted to the airport, he flew back to Halifax, not on his own power, but by plane, because there is a well-known proverb, "Coughing angels never fly."

So Murray's and my curiosity was satisfied as to

what an archangel was. We had almost gagged one. We never heard from the archangel after this. We felt he should have kept in touch. However from time to time we heard rumours that he was hovering somewhere over Halifax, still coughing, but unable to come in for a landing because of the fog (which was hard on his sinuses).

On The Third Day It Will Arise

When Ma died, all the household tasks fell to us four. One day shortly before Christmas, while visiting next door and borrowing a cup of sugar, a sweet elderly lady called Nan gave me a piece of her plum bread. It tasted delicious, much tastier than our large loaves of white bread. Nan said, "Andy dear, it's not hard to make, I'll give you the recipe." I wasn't going to tell anyone at home that I was going to make plum bread, instead of white. It was to be kind of a Christmas surprise. I hardly needed the recipe, as for a few years I had been baking white bread once a week, with Murray baking the other day.

On a cold morning in December I got my large bread pan, and five large sifters of flour were shaken around. Then I threw in the extra ingredients, molasses, raisins, cinnamon, etc. Kneading them all together, I placed the batch on the oven door of the old coal stove.

Used to this twice weekly, my brothers and Pa weren't surprised to see bread waiting to rise, but they never had a clue it was plum bread. I had mixed it at eight a.m. but at ten p.m. that night it was still as flat as a man's chest. My brothers were amazed that I didn't have about twenty loaves cooked and cooling off on the old cupboard sideboard, as the white bread was getting scarce for Pa's lunch can at this time.

After patiently waiting this long, and hoping for a miracle, I began to realize my mistake. The flour, which was kept in our porch, was ice cold when I mixed it, and the raisins and molasses were holding it down. It didn't even look as though it would be ready for next Christmas. But I wasn't telling anyone, especially Pa, as he'd say, "Why didn't you make white bread? it's cheaper." I was determined to go through with the planned surprise, even if I had to have the batch of dough inseminated so it would become pregnant. I shoved another sweater underneath the pan, which already had three Macknaws and a woolen blanket over it, another reason why no one knew it was plum bread. It would have taken them a quarter of an hour to relieve the clothes I had smothered it with.

The old kitchen stove had been banked with damp coal around ten p.m., so I transferred the stubborn bread to the fireplace in the front room, which still had a few glows of burning coal in it.

At five a.m. after Pa left for work, I looked at my bread again. There was positively no change, in fact it looked as though it was becoming mummified. Billy told me later that he had just used the last loaf of white bread, which meant there would be none for Pa's lunch can. If I'd had any other mixing utensils, I would have whipped up a white batch, but there was nothing left to use but the pot. As much as Pa hated Baker's fog in his lunch, there was no alternative but to buy a loaf. Arriving from the mine that same day at suppertime, you could see by the look on Pa's face something had gone wrong, as he walked slowly into the porch with a "Who put that poison bread in my lunch? I've been having heartburn all day."

Late that second evening there was no change in the

bread, so I went up to our neighbour Nan's to get some help. Being of Scottish descent, she said, "Put some more yeast in it, begory. Just dissolve it and pat it around the bread, begory." At eight p.m. the second night I put the yeast to it, twice the amount she told me, as this was becoming a crisis. She told me to keep it good and warm, and it would have to rise. If this didn't work, and had I been a chemist, I could have pumped it full of helium, and Pa could become a blimp.

I remedied Pa's heartburn by making a bran cake in twenty minutes that night, and he took the whole thing in his lunch can as he loved bran cakes.

On the third day, I unravelled the coats, blankets, sweaters etc., to see if there was any change. What a relief, finally the bread was rising. I took it from the fireplace, and placed it in an old chesterfield chair—I was told to keep it cosy, and this was the cosiest chair in the house—and I put back the coverings. Rising about a foot by three p.m., I pushed down the first rise, because this made the bread lighter. What a spot I had for it, close to the kitchen fire, lots of heat and snuggled up good and warm. The next rise was the time to pan it.

Pa arrived at five p.m., and it was always his custom to read the evening paper before supper, in the rocking chair. But this evening Pa was comfortably reading his paper, sitting not in the rocking chair, but on the tired-out bread in the chesterfield chair. Relaxed, with a contented look on his face, he had settled into the softest cushion known to man. We four brothers knew what was happening, but there was nothing we could do. I took the odd look to see if Pa had risen an inch or so since he was seated, as all that yeast was really working now. It was the first time Pa had said he'd wait for awhile for supper, as he wasn't too hungry, and he proceeded to settle even deeper into my Christmas surprise.

We were sorry for the bread, which had just gotten the gumption to rise, when Pa's two-hundred-and-fifty-pound frame had squashed it back down again. We tried to coax Pa to the table, saying we had his favourite salt herring, but he must have been getting a lift and a drop at the same time because he had a sweet look on his face, as though he could sleep there.

It was now seven p.m., and it looked as though I'd be up until four a.m. baking bread. Finally at seven-thirty p.m. Pa slid off the bread pan and took his place at the head of the table to eat his supper.

Had strangers been to our house after Pa left the chair and believed in ghosts, they wouldn't have stayed too long, as in the direction of the chair sweaters, coats, blankets were rising at the rate of six inches an hour.

Pa never noticed the plum loaf, and the bodyguard we had arranged for when Pa finished eating quickly blocked off that big chair, so Pa had no alternative but to advance instead to the rocking chair, or to be thrown to the floor by Billy in a judo hold.

My brothers had also arranged the rocker so Pa couldn't see the eruption taking place while he was having his after-supper pipe smoke. Almost chasing Pa to bed, I had a busy night ahead. As I cut off mounds of dough, Teedy, Billy and Murray had a surprised look on their face and said, "Oh, it's plum bread, no wonder you had so much trouble." Had I let it continue rising, we might have had to call Pa down next morning from the attic instead of his bedroom, as it would have lifted him, bed, ceiling and all right up there.

In greased pans, waiting for another rise, the next

169

day at three p.m. the last loaf was transferred from the oven. Next day Pa said he liked the bread, and wondered who had made it. I felt like saying, "Pa it would have been a hell of a lot better if you hadn't sat on it for three hours. At least I'd have had more sleep." But casually I told him I thought we had needed a change, and he seemed to be quite satisfied.

Those twenty loaves only lasted a day, and Murray's turn to bake came a day earlier. I never attempted to make plum bread again, as it took three nights and three days tending it like a sick child. But Pa never looked as comfortable as when he was sitting on the bread that night. After this, he never had that *umph* feeling and never again made such a big impression on my bread.

Don't Slip On The Soap

Four times a week our hardwood floor in the kitchen had to be scrubbed. There was no way to get clear of this job unless Pa won a maid at a card party. The kitchen was about twelve by sixteen and held six hardwood chairs, a square table and the big coal stove. Water was heated on the stove in the huge pot that my red cap fit over, and as the floor had never been sanded or varnished, it took many pots of hot water to scrub it. We should have hired witches for this job. They were used to working with cauldrons.

An old coat was placed under our knees, as we'd all heard of housemaid's knee and we didn't want to be the only males blessed with that. But with all the women's tasks we performed after Ma died, it's a wonder we didn't end up with the whole body of a housemaid. Why, Murray at the age of fourteen had swollen breasts, and if it hadn't been for the black salve Dr. Archibald prescribed, Murray would have had to wear a brassiere and would have shamed us while we were swimming for the rest of our lives.

A galvanized bucket was taken from the small porch and filled to about three-quarters full with hot water. Then a pound of P&G soap was unwrapped and most of the pound was used. Old Dutch Cleanser was sprinkled on our young Canadian dirt on a square about three-by-three feet, or as far as the arm could reach with a six-inch scrub brush without becoming dislocated from its sockets. With the chairs out in the hall I had clear sailing. I liked to do this cleaning while alone, but there was always one brother watching to see if it was the way he'd done it. Fist fights would erupt at times when someone walked on your cleaned patch before it was dried.

Billy was the worst of all. He could get that floor the whitest and we all told him why. He wasn't a bit saving on the soap and Dutch Cleanser, and we were. We hated when it was Billy's turn to scrub as he was too strict with us. Once he'd finished the floor, he expected us to fly around the kitchen like Mighty Mouse hours after he'd finished scrubbing. Billy had a lot of Pa in him in this respect. He'd even throw a couple of lefts if he saw us walking on his floor the day he scrubbed. When he saw one of us coming up the street, he'd open the porch door, shouting, "Take your shoes off," whatever the season.

Never dreaming what a dangerous weapon the soap could be, each of us would try to save on it and would slide it along outside the bucket, all except for Billy who I think washed himself with it at the same time.

It was my turn to scrub this day. With about two squares left and still using my third water, I surveyed my floor. It was beginning to dry with a snow-white appearance. Thinking I should change to the fourth water to give the remainder of the floor the same snow-white effect before the seven dwarfs came home, I got to my feet and proceeded to the huge pot which was boiling furiously. (If only we could have cooked Pa in that.) Dumping in some cold water to cool it a bit, I filled my scrub-pail three-quarters full.

With a firm grip on my pail of water and my knee pad, the old coat slung over my shoulders, I dashed back to finish my job. In my rush the coat sleeve flapped across my face, blinding me, and my next trick was to tramp on the soap. Had I just stepped on it and stumbled, it wouldn't have been so bad. But I had bigger plans. I took the weight off the foot that was soapless and transferred all my weight to the cake of soap. The slippery wet soap acted like a skate, while I balanced, steering my body with great effort as though on a skateboard. With this heavy steering, I managed to skate on one foot past the kitchen window, still hanging onto the bucket and contents. Two strong men couldn't have thrown me harder into the corner of that house. I skidded with a thud against the wall. As I lost my grip, the bucket smashed against the wall, splashing water to the ceiling and streaming it across my clean floor. I held onto everything and almost drowned myself in the corner. Now I'd have to tell Pa that either the house had caught fire and the firemen had hosed down the kitchen, or that an escaped elephant had slipped through the door and let go with a trunk-load of water.

For minutes I didn't realize what was hurting me most, until I touched my ear. I had hit the side of my head on the empty bucket that was now sitting erect with not a drop of water in it. My ear, bruised considerably, swelled up as big as a catcher's mitt. It could have been worse though. Had I not directed my trip as I slipped along, I might have crashed right through the window, out into the yard and down to the little corner grocery store.

Dazed, I gave a faint call to Teedy, who was out in the hallway. Surprised to see me in a heap on the floor, he asked, "What'd ya do?" "I don't know yet, but I think I've been decapitated and I just might be growing a housemaid's knee on my ear."

He could see my ear swelling up fast, and since Pa would be home from the mine in a half hour he rushed over and grabbed an old floor cloth and began soaking up the water. Peeping over the corner of my swollen ear, I saw Teedy drop to his knees, praying fashion, and I prayed that he said one for me as I was still tangled up in my knee pad in the corner. I arose and limped towards him to drop the old coat down for his knees, because I didn't want Teedy to get that knee either. He had enough to contend with with his Charlie Brown head. Automatically he tucked the coat beneath him and scrubbed over the last two patches.

It was Teedy's turn to get supper so I took a wet towel and slithered upstairs, acutely aware of the huge ear that was beginning to get in the way of my eye. I began to think I might need an operation to let the air out of my ear. Pa wouldn't even need his reading glasses to check an ear this size for cleanliness. While I was upstairs soaking my ear, Teedy arrived and said with great pity, "You'll have to help me with the scrubbing Wednesday." Peering at him over my ear, with half a smile, I whispered, "You watch out for the elephants and I'll carry the soap. Better still, if Pa's not home, we'll let the soap stay in the water, as next time I might not be so lucky—I might slip right out through the door, over the cliff and into the ocean, and with all that soap and all that water, I'd probably slide through the Bermuda Triangle right down to China."

Look At That Thing Go
But there was nothing compared to cockroaches. Vicious dogs and even a saucy bull didn't give me as terrifying a feeling as did a cockroach. And each encounter I had with them always caught me by surprise.

We hardly ever had them at home, unless Pa brought one home from the mine in his lunch-can. The washhouse at the mine was a good place to get them where the men changed and bathed before coming home. No one in the house was brave about those cockroaches. Rather than tramping them to death, or slapping them down with a paper, we would have used a grenade when one appeared.

One time Billy gave me a beautiful suit that was too small for him. It originally came from California. Some relative of ours had died. He was cold only ten minutes when a sister sent Billy one of his suits, and though he loved the suit, he was just too large for it. He would have worn it though if he could have found someone to follow him around to help him lift his arms up. The cuffs of the coat sleeves were six inches above his wrist, clinging to him like a straightjacket. The relative must have had tiny arms the length of a soup ladle. Even for me, the arms were four inches too short. But it was green silk and, except for the sleeves, it fit me tip-top. I knew it had to be good because even a piece of twine coming from the U.S.A. seemed better than ours.

I loved it even when it was hanging in the closet. With that suit on, I was in a different world, leaving my poorly clothed brothers down on a plateau by themselves.

174

I wanted no harm to ever come to that suit. Sitting or standing I was always prepared to protect it from attack or any sudden tangle or catch, and if I had been attacked by a mugger, my only request would have been, "You may kill me, but don't lay a finger on the suit."

One Saturday morning in a restaurant I used to frequent, I was at my highest peak. A free morning paper was on the table to my left. Before ordering a five-cent cup of coffee, I extended my handsomely garbed arm, with the lights of the restaurant flickering over the different silk threads of the short coat sleeve. It was a shame there weren't mirrors placed all around me so I could have seen more of my beautifully clad body. I even assumed difficult twists to my body at the exact moment someone was looking—to show them the textures and richness of my dead friend's suit.

Now there was only one other customer in the restaurant, the owner of a loan office in town. Needless to say, a stranger visiting the restaurant would have picked me as the president of the loan company, with my lovely silk suit on, instead of the owner with his cheap woolen suit, his arms not glistening at all.

The waitress, arriving with my lonely order, sat it on my table, which was next to the window and close to the wall. The loan shark sat at his table in the centre of the restaurant, making me ill at ease as he spread his six-foot body into the aisle to advertise size thirteen shoes, and digging into his full breakfast of ham and eggs.

I proceeded to divide the paper into sections, to pick my favourite pages. My right hand was toward the window and somehow clasped inside my coat pocket. My coffee was sending up steam signals, cooling off, as I gave a fast hunch to my shoulders to iron out any possible wrinkles in my suit.

Tearing my eyes away from my suit and looking straight ahead down the hall-like entrance facing me, I suddenly saw my foe arriving, coming up fast. A cockroach as big as a small mouse was looking as though it had no one on its mind but me. As it came closer, I prepared to defend myself. Up flew both my feet, coming to rest on the top of my table. The loan shark's feet were still flung out in the aisle. How I wished this monster would reroute its course toward him. I breathed a sigh of relief as I saw it put its tall legs into another gear and without putting on its turn signal go straight towards the moneylender. Down came my legs as I relaxed with another sip of coffee.

My gaze now went from my paper over to the lanky loan shark. Had he been of a friendly nature, I would have warned him of the roach. But, knowing the man and his attitude toward the lower classes, I was hoping it would crawl up his neck, into his mouth, and come out through his ear. Half smiling, I scanned his boots while he was busy pouring over the stock quotations. I wondered when the roach would reach him.

I went back to my coffee to enjoy reading about a UFO sighted in Texas. Reaching for another sip, my head nearly flew off my shoulders. I had made the big mistake of not keeping an eye on the cockroach, as it had changed its course again, come back to me, and crawled up the wall next to my window where the law of gravity had taken hold. The beast's body landed with a splash in my remaining coffee.

I couldn't get my hand out of my pocket fast enough, and ended up completely ripping the pocket off my lovely silk suit. The waitress, a few feet from my table, heard me as I hollered, "Here comes a cockroach!" and was killing herself laughing at the actions I was going through to get rid of it. I was now thankful they hadn't called people in off the street to feast their eyes on my suit. The laughter would have been deafening.

Then the finance man began to laugh. This was the last straw, as I was mad at him for letting the roach come back in my direction. Needing to satisfy my anger, I looked in his direction and said, "You don't seem to be scared of them. That leads me to believe your house is alive with them," assuring him the only ones we had home were ones who got a free ride home from the pit in Pa's lunch can. But he never said a word—just looked at me as though I was a lunatic.

I still wasn't finished with him, after looking down at my priceless suit. I asked him if he wanted the roach in *his* coffee. He ignored me and continued reading. I was thinking I should go over and tear *his* pockets off, but that wouldn't have put him out any, as he probably had a dozen more suits.

I even made a trip to the manager and showed him my damage, only to get another good laugh. He told me that Lloyds of London were deciding on an insurance policy for humans who were assaulted by roaches.

I left the restaurant in my glistening, pocketless suit, fantasizing that the next time I visited that place I would come equipped with a large trap, one which would catch not only cockroaches, but loan sharks.

These embarrassing incidents have followed me around throughout my life—and the more I try to get ahead, the more behind I get. But I keep plugging away, bright-eyed and bushy-tailed, over hill and dale, laughing and scratching. . . .